CLASSICAL GREECE

TIME
LIFE
BOOKS

GREAT AGES OF MAN
A History of the World's Cultures

CLASSICAL GREECE

by

C. M. BOWRA

and

The Editors of TIME-LIFE Books

TIME INCORPORATED, NEW YORK

THE AUTHOR: C. M. Bowra is warden of Wadham College at Oxford, and a towering figure in classical studies. He has held the vice-chancellorship of the University, Oxford's highest academic post. Among his books are *Tradition and Design in the Iliad, Early Greek Elegists, Sophoclean Tragedy,* as well as *The Greek Experience,* which won him a wide audience. Sir Maurice has also translated Pindar's Pythian Odes and been a co-editor of *The Oxford Book of Greek Verse in Translation.*

THE CONSULTING EDITOR: Leonard Krieger, formerly Professor of History at Yale, now holds the post of University Professor at the University of Chicago. He is the author of *The German Idea of Freedom* and *Politics of Discretion.*

THE COVER: This head is part of a statue of Poseidon that probably dates from the middle of the Fifth Century B.C. It was found in the Aegean in the 1920s.

TIME-LIFE BOOKS

EDITOR
Norman P. Ross
TEXT DIRECTOR   ART DIRECTOR
William Jay Gold   Edward A. Hamilton
CHIEF OF RESEARCH
Beatrice T. Dobie
Assistant Text Director: Jerry Korn
Assistant Art Director: Arnold Holeywell
Assistant Chief of Research: Monica O. Horne

PUBLISHER
Rhett Austell
General Manager: Joseph C. Hazen Jr.
Business Manager: John D. McSweeney
Circulation Manager: Joan D. Manley

GREAT AGES OF MAN

SERIES EDITOR: Harold C. Field
Editorial Staff for *Classical Greece:*
Assistant to the Editor: Peter Meyerson
Text Editor: Betsy Frankel
Designer: Norman Snyder
Staff Writer: John Stanton
Chief Researcher: Carlotta Kerwin
Researchers:
Terry Drucker
Dori Watson, Lilla Zabriskie
Barbara Moir, Linda Wolfe

EDITORIAL PRODUCTION
Color Director: Robert L. Young
Art Assistants: James D. Smith, Wayne R. Young,
David Wyland
Picture Researchers: Margaret K. Goldsmith,
Joan T. Lynch
Copy Staff: Marian Gordon Goldman,
Rosalind Stubenberg, Dolores A. Littles

Valuable aid in preparing this book was given by Doris O'Neil, Chief, LIFE Picture Library; Content Peckham, Chief, Time Inc. Bureau of Editorial Reference; Richard M. Clurman, Chief, TIME-LIFE News Service; Correspondents Helga Kohl (Athens), Ann Natanson and Joseph Pilcher (Rome), Katharine Sachs (London), Elisabeth Kraemer (Bonn), Franz Spelman (Munich), Gertraud Lessing (Vienna) and Joseph Harriss (Paris).

CONTENTS

INTRODUCTION

Apart from its other claims to fame, the importance assigned by Classical Greece to individual achievement assures it a place among the great ages of man. There were earlier great ages, but those periods were dominated for the most part by absolute rulers of monolithic states; the truly creative individuals who certainly existed in Egypt, Mesopotamia and Anatolia are almost entirely anonymous.

Classical Greece was different. We know the names of more than 20,000 individuals in Athens alone, most of them recorded because of their participation in civic affairs. Recent excavations in the heart of Athens have yielded over a thousand *ostraka* (the potsherds, or pottery fragments, that gave their name to the institution of ostracism), each bearing the name of some outstanding man— Aristides, Themistocles, Cimon, Pericles and many others. Each *ostrakon* offers proof that at some stage in their careers the men were suspected by their fellow citizens of aiming at tyranny. These *ostraka* remind us that the Athenians were ever mindful of the need to maintain a balance between personal ambition and the civic interest.

In other aspects of life, we find that the beginnings of the various literary genres, of the schools of philosophy, of the major artistic trends are all associated with individual men. Even in the crafts the individual stands out. The fine pottery made in Athens in the Sixth and Fifth Centuries B.C. can be assigned to some five hundred different masters, many of whom signed their products.

To this emphasis on the individual man Greek history owes much of its sparkling and perpetual human interest. For this reason, too, that study may be salutary for our own society, all too prone to accept regimentation and nameless conformity.

The distinguished Commission on the Humanities, established in 1963 by three of the leading scholarly organizations in the United States, has stated:

> *Even the most gifted individual, whether poet or physicist, will not realize his full potential or make his fullest contribution to his times unless his imagination has been kindled by the aspirations and accomplishments of those who have gone before him. Humanist scholars have therefore . . . the privilege and obligation of interpreting the past to each new generation of men who 'necessarily must live in one small corner for one little stretch of time.'*

This book in the TIME-LIFE series on the Great Ages of Man makes important contributions to the achievement of these goals. Its author is a happy choice. Sir Maurice Bowra has devoted his life to the contemplation of Greek literature, art and society. His brilliant distillation of Hellenism on the following pages shows us Greece in all its dewy freshness. In the picture essays that document various aspects of the Greek experience, even the most assiduous reader of the current spate of books on Greece will discover much that is new and refreshing, imaginatively deployed to bring out the essence of Classical Greece.

HOMER A. THOMPSON
Field Director, American School of Classical Studies at Athens

ALPS

ADRIATIC SEA

PAEONIA

BALKAN

MACEDONIA

ILLYRIA

Epidamnus

STRYMON R.

AXIUS R.

Pella

Amphipolis

EPIRUS

Dodona

THESSALY

MT. OLYMPUS

HALIACMON R.

Olynthus

CHALCIDICE

Potidaea

CORCYRA

PINDUS MTS.

PENEUS R.

Larissa

IONIAN SEA

Ambracia

Pharsalus

MAGNESIA

Pagasae

NORTHERN SPORADES

LEUCAS

ACARNANIA

AETOLIA

MT. PARNASSUS

MALIS

DORIS

SCYROS

ITHACA

LOCRIS OZOLIS

Delphi

LOCRIS

EUBOEA

CEPHALONIA

MT. CYLLENE

PHOCIS

BOEOTIA

Thebes

Chalcis

ACHAEA

CORINTHIAN GULF

Sicyon

Corinth

ATTICA

AEGEAN

ELIS

Megara

Eleusis

ZACYNTHUS

Olympia

ARCADIA

Mycenae

Piraeus

Athens

ANDROS

Tegea

Argos

Epidaurus

AEGINA

Megalopolis

Tiryns

Troezen

SARONIC GULF

Messene

Sparta

ARGOLIS

Pylos

TAYGETUS MTS.

EUROTAS R.

LACONIA

CYCLADES

DELOS

MESSENIA

PELOPONNESUS

SIPHNOS

PAROS

NAXOS

CYTHERA

MELOS

CRETE

Cnossus

MEDITERRANEAN SEA

LAND OF THE GREEKS

1

CRADLE OF
THE MODERN SPIRIT

For centuries Greece has exerted a peculiar enchantment over the imaginations of men. The Romans, who incorporated Greece into their empire—and in the process did not shrink from sacking its cities—were deeply impressed by it. Young Romans were sent to study at the university in Athens, and educated Romans looked to the Greeks as their masters in philosophy, science and the fine arts. Despite the Romans' confidence in their own imperial mission and their gift for government, they felt, a little uneasily, that there was much in art, letters and thought which they could never hope to do as well as the Greeks.

When the Italian Renaissance of the 15th Century A.D. brought an intensified interest in the ancient world, Rome at first held the attention. But behind the imposing Roman façade, scholars and poets felt the presence of something more powerful and more alluring. Slowly this was disentangled from the mists of the past, and the full majesty of the Greek performance was revealed. So great was Greek prestige that Greek ideas on medicine, astronomy and geography were accepted with unquestioning faith until the 17th Century, when the birth of a new scientific spirit inaugurated the era of experiment and inquiry into which we ourselves have been born.

Even today, when we have discarded so many creeds and cosmologies, the Greek view of life excites and exalts us. Greek thought and Greek assumptions are closely woven into the fabric of our lives almost without our knowing it, and for this reason alone we are right to wish to know about the Greeks, to assess the value and the scope of their achievement. No people can afford to neglect its own origins, and the modern world is far too deeply indebted to Greece to accept in unthinking ingratitude what it has inherited.

At the center of the Greek outlook lay an unshakable belief in the worth of the individual man. In centuries when large parts of the earth were dominated by the absolute monarchies of the east, the Greeks were evolving their belief that a man must be respected not as the instrument of an omnipotent overlord, but for his own sake. They sought at all costs to be themselves, and in this they were helped by the nature of their country.

PALLAS ATHENA *was a goddess with many roles, among others protectress of civilized life and donor of the indispensable olive tree. In this statue she is shown in her helmet, garbed as the defender of righteous causes.*

EVOLVING STYLES *in portraying the male form, the central figure in Greek art, are shown here. They began with the nearly abstract (1000-700 B.C.), on the left, went through the stiff, monumental kind of figure (700-500 B.C.) in the center and finally reached the graceful naturalism of the statue (500-300 B.C.) at the right.*

GEOMETRIC PERIOD

Geographically, Greece was in ancient times very much what it is today: the southernmost extremity of the huge Balkan mass. A land of hard limestone mountains separated by deep valleys, it is cut almost in two by the narrow divide of the Corinthian Gulf. To the east the structure of the mainland is continued intermittently by islands, and the whole pattern is rounded off to the south by the long rampart of Crete, which has been called "the stepping-stone of continents." Even including the islands, Greece is a small country, smaller than Yemen or Florida. Moreover, this small area has never been able to support more than a few million inhabitants, and yet in the history of Western civilization it has played an enormous part.

The reason is partly geographical. In Egypt and Mesopotamia, in the great riverlands of the Nile and the Euphrates, it was easy to subject a large population to a single ruler and to see that each man performed an allotted function in a vast, unified system. But in Greece, where every district was separated from the next by mountains or the sea, central control of this kind was impossible, and men were forced to be not specialists in this or that profession but masters of a whole range of crafts and accomplishments. Each separate group was deeply aware of its own being, and within each group its members were cognizant of their responsibilities. The Greek climate, dry and exhilarating and gifted with the most magical of skies, incited to action, while the sea, which was always at hand, developed in its servants an unusual skill of both hand and eye.

Nature nursed the Greeks in a hard school, but this made them conscious of themselves and their worth. Without this self-awareness they would never have made their most important contribution to human experience: the belief that a man must be honored for his individual worth and treated with respect just because he is himself. In the words of the great Athenian statesman Pericles: "Each single one of our citizens, in all the manifold aspects of life, is able to show himself the rightful lord and owner of his own person, and do this, moreover, with exceptional grace and exceptional versatility."

This is what the Greeks meant by liberty. Just as they detested the thought of being conquered, so in their own circles a man claimed for himself the freedom to do all of which he was capable, to realize his full potential within his society, to speak what was in his mind, to go his own way without interference from other men. The belief in freedom was sustained by a deep respect for personal honor, and nurtured by a love for action.

This feeling among the Greeks may have started as something vague, but it was deeply felt, and it matured into reasoned philosophy which long after shaped, and still shapes, our own. Supported by ethical and psychological arguments, it was based on convictions which we take so much for granted today that we can hardly imagine what efforts must have been made to establish the philosophy, or what its absence meant outside Greece. It had its own dangers, of course, especially the risk that in

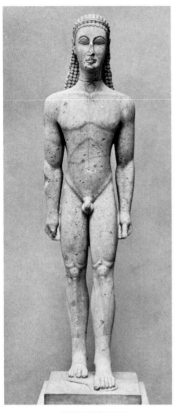

ARCHAIC PERIOD   CLASSICAL PERIOD

asserting their own claims men would pay too little attention to their neighbors' and reduce society to anarchy. And indeed Greek states did suffer gravely from internal dissensions. Nevertheless they survived as centers of order—because the Greek belief in liberty was inextricably associated with the existence of law.

The Greeks did not invent law or originate the notion of it. Codes of law existed in Babylonia when the Greeks were still little better than savages, and the Mosaic Law of Israel is also ancient. But Greek law, which emerged in the Seventh Century B.C., differed from these in several respects. First, it was not intended to carry out the will either of an omnipotent monarch or of a god; Greek law aimed entirely at improving the lot of mortal humans. Second, while these earlier systems could be changed virtually at the will of a king or a priesthood, Greek law was usually based on some kind of popular consent and could be changed only by being referred to the people for their approval. Finally, Greek law was expected to secure life and property for all members of a society, not just for a select group of leaders or priests. The Greeks

regarded themselves as vastly superior in this respect to the Persians, who, utterly dependent on their king's whim, were in the Greek view no better than slaves.

From the first Greek lawgivers stems the whole majestic succession of the West's legal systems. The Romans, great lawmakers in their own right, learned from the Greeks. In turn, the comprehensive codes of Gaius and Justinian gave rise to most modern legal systems.

The belief in law emphasized and strengthened an ethnic pride which shaped the whole political development of the Greeks. A Greek state consisted of a city and of the lands around it which provided its livelihood. Each state formed its own habits, rules and government; as a consequence local loyalties were remarkably strong. But beyond this, the Greeks had a second loyalty, vaguer perhaps and not always paramount, but in the end irresistible. Though they quarreled and fought with one another, they felt strongly that they were all Greeks, men who spoke some form of the same language, worshiped the same gods and obeyed the same customs—and in all these respects they saw themselves as vastly superior to other races or nations. Though they never created a truly national state such as those of the modern world, they presented a strong contrast to the multinational empires of Babylonia or Persia, which comprised a large number of different peoples held together not because they shared a common culture or ideal but simply because they were subjects of a despotic ruler. Whenever the Greeks were attacked by a foreign enemy, they fought against him to defend their Greek heritage as well as their local liberties.

The Greeks' sense of personal achievement, of a man's obligation to make the most of his natural gifts, led them to give to the works of their hands the same care and attention that they gave to the structure of political life. In the Greek view, any-

thing worth doing was worth doing well, and the remains of their humblest pots have a remarkable distinction. Even objects so utilitarian as coins are little masterpieces of relief sculpture in gold or silver.

We may ask why so much of the Greeks' work, which has survived the centuries by accident and is therefore truly representative of what they did, has so high a quality, so fine a design. The answer is partly that the Greek artisans worked for specific patrons instead of manufacturing wholesale for an anonymous public. The patrons (who included the state) knew what they wanted and insisted on getting it. The Greeks wanted their arts and handicrafts to stand the acid tests of time and to keep their attraction for future generations; in this fashion they hoped to prolong their own influence into the future. In addition, they had a strong desire to impose order on any disordered mass of material, such as rock or clay in its natural state. Not content to leave things as they found them, they wished to rearrange and shape them. But they employed restraint in this process, and the result has that quality of balance and completeness which we call classical.

In the major arts, notably in sculpture, this sense of fine workmanship was inspired and reinforced by something more exalted. Greek sculpture was meant to be seen in public places, principally in temples, and it had to be worthy of the gods. It had to have a nobility and dignity, and yet it could not be too remote from everyday things, for in these the gods were believed to be always at work. All this explains why Greek art at its best never aimed

at violent, gross or grotesque effects. Instead it showed men in the full strength of their lithe, muscular bodies, women in the rippling drapery of their finest clothes.

When Greek art dealt with animals, as it often did, it displayed dogs alert to every scent and sound, lions leaping on their prey with savage mastery, horses elegantly on the move. This art found its material in the real world, but the artist felt that to do justice to what he saw, he must impart to it an order and balance. What was true of high sculpture was no less true of humbler arts such as decorations on pottery. The explanation in each case is that art was intended to perpetuate something visible by revealing what was most important in it.

The Greeks were a people who lacked inhibitions in speaking about themselves, and as might be expected, they delighted in words. They had at their disposal a wonderfully subtle, expressive and adaptable language, and they made full use of it. With the Greeks, as with many peoples, poetry came before prose. Poetry, in fact, became almost a second religion, and it was created with all the care and insight that was accorded to the visual arts. Poets

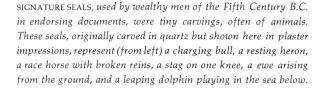

were highly esteemed—a poet, said the philosopher Socrates, was "a light and winged and holy thing" —and they wrote about all sorts of subjects: farming, local lore, the weather. If a man, any man, had something important to say he often said it in verse —which in the early days meant that he said it in song, for almost all Greek poetry was originally sung or spoken to music.

Poetry was the Greeks' immediate response to a wide range of experience, and to reflect this variety they invented or perfected many of the poetic forms we now know. They seem to have begun with the heroic epic, which is objective storytelling in verse of exciting and tragic events. They followed this with a more personal, more emotional poetry, which was sung to the lyre and is called lyric for this reason. At their high noon the Greeks invented both tragedy and comedy, the first dealing with the darker and more difficult relations between the gods and men, the second viewing with derisive ribaldry all manner of human foibles. Even in later years they continued to write charming poetry, though its strength had become diminished and its subjects less majestic.

The most striking quality of Greek literature, poetry and prose alike, is that it is as alive and relevant today as it was when it was first written. We cannot fail to respond to the extraordinary power with which it presents issues of perennial urgency. We may admire it for its technical skill, but what binds us to it is its profound humanity, its wise appreciation of human values. It deals with precise issues in a universal way, and it gains our attention not by arguing for this side or for that but by presenting a situation in full, in all its powerful implications. Its extraordinary immediacy and directness drive home its imaginative thoughts with an irresistible power, and behind it we feel the living force of people who were eager to examine their destinies with the utmost candor and passion.

The arts were not the only creative fields in which the Greeks excelled. The nature of the physical world excited their curiosity and led them to make spectacular scientific hypotheses. Before them, to be sure, much of a practical nature had been accomplished in such fields as astronomy and engineering by Egyptians and Babylonians. The Greeks' unique contribution was to provide a theoretical basis for these applied sciences. They sought general principles, and in the process became not only the founders of science but of philosophy (literally, "love of knowledge"). To the Greeks the two fields were closely related, both being means by which men could seek to find out more about the nature of things, and both moving by argument and proof from one hypothesis to another.

If in their practical way the Greeks needed astronomy for navigation and an understanding of

THE OLYMPIAN GODS *in this procession are, from the left: Persephone; Hermes; Aphrodite; Ares; Demeter with wheat sheaves; Hephaestus; Hera with scepter; Poseidon with his trident; Athena with a spear; Zeus, chief of the gods, with his thunderbolt; Artemis with bow; and Apollo. The Greeks revised the membership list of this pantheon at times.*

weights and stresses for building, they strengthened and broadened this technical knowledge with theories and general principles about the nature of matter and space and motion, which they expressed in mathematics, especially in geometry. Then they often reaped the benefits in other fields: Pythagoras set a firm foundation for music, for example, by discovering the numerical ratios of the lengths of string that would produce a seven-note scale.

While Greek science was developing on a theoretical basis, it also saw the need for observation and experiment. When medicine flowered in the Fifth Century B.C. under the inspiration of the great physician Hippocrates of Cos, it made its first task the collection of data from which deductions could be drawn. Thus in the identification of diseases a Greek doctor set great store on the correct description of symptoms, and proceeded from that point to do what he could to effect a cure. Medicine was of course very much in its infancy, and doctors were much better at diagnosing a complaint than in knowing what to do for it, but at least they had made a great advance over the old days when illnesses were thought to be curable by amulets, magic charms and the like. In surgéry the beginnings were primitive enough, but by experimenting

on animals and learning something about the principles of physiology, the Greeks were able to deal with fractures and dislocations, which were common among athletes, and with wounds—especially head wounds—received in war.

The spirit which inspired Greek researches into nature was also at work on human actions, and it made the Greeks the first true historians. Their accounts of past events gradually changed from legend to verifiable fact; "What I write here," said Hecataeus of Miletus at the beginning of the Fifth Century B.C., "is the account of what I thought to be true; for the stories of the Greeks [of other centuries] are numerous, and in my opinion ridiculous."

In pursuing truth for its own sake the Greeks were hampered by no rigid theology. Since they were not tied to creeds, they were free to ask questions about the scheme of things. Such inquiries, far from being thought impious, were often regarded as a quasi-religious activity because they showed the wonderful workings of the gods. As the philosopher Xenophanes said, "The gods did not reveal everything to men at the beginning, but men, as they seek in time, find something better." Thales, a thoroughly rational man, who was able to foretell an eclipse in 585 B.C., nevertheless insisted

that "all things are full of gods," and this was the usual Greek attitude.

Thus Greek art and Greek science fitted in happily with Greek religion; indeed, religion did much to inspire and sustain the poets and philosophers. Though Greek gods might seem to modern minds often to fall below the standards demanded of divinity, they had something impressive in common. They were all to a high degree embodiments of power, whether in the physical world or in the mind of man. From them came literally everything, both visible and invisible, and it was the task of the mortals to make the proper use of what the gods provided.

The Greeks took all the familiar steps to keep in contact with their gods. They offered prayers and hymns and sacrifices; they consulted all kinds of oracles; they had countless shrines containing images of the gods. They hoped that the gods would be kind to them, and they spoke of them in the language of friendship. They had no very clear doctrines. Even on the subject of life after death they varied from thinking that the dead were unsubstantial ghosts to imagining an Elysium beyond the Western Sea. They felt the gods' presence everywhere, especially in times of need such as battle, but equally on high occasions of festival and rejoicing. They thought the gods far more beautiful than men could ever hope to be, and they did not expect them to follow the rules of human behavior. What counted was their power.

Because the gods were the sources of power, men honored every kind of power and wished to display it in their own lives. This applied equally to war, the arts, athletic games and thought. If a Greek did well in any of these, he was making a proper use of his divinely provided gifts and to that extent he was getting nearer to the gods. This is what Aristotle means when he says: "We must be immortal as far as we can." Thus the Greeks stood in an ambivalent relation to their gods, at once eager to be as much like them as possible, yet knowing that humans must not attempt this too eagerly, lest they imagine that they were gods.

This ambivalence proved of great value. From it came the characteristic Greek mixture of energy and moderation, both in life and the arts. While the Greeks zestfully tried every form of action, they tempered it with the maxim "Nothing in excess," and they praised the desirability of the Mean, the middle state between attempting too much and not attempting enough. Needless to say, they did not always achieve the Mean, but it was at least an ideal, and it set its mark on their civilization. They felt in themselves a driving strength which came from the gods, and they knew that it was their task to make the most of this, not by seeking pleasure and sensation (though of course they enjoyed these as the reward for their efforts) but by shaping their lives to rational and desirable ends. As the Greeks set out to make the best of their natural gifts and to be worthy of their human nature, they dedicated themselves to noble toil, to creating something new and splendid, to keeping their bodies as fit as their minds, to making order out of disorder, and to living in harmony with their fellow citizens.

THE GREAT LEGACY

"Future ages will wonder at us,
as the present age wonders at us now"

ANCIENT GREECE left some of the most magnificent works of art and literary monuments ever bequeathed by one civilization to another. But it is not mostly for these that the legacy of Greece is great. It is, rather, because of the spirit they evoke, a spirit rooted in the belief that man is a free, indeed an exalted, being. For thousands of years older civilizations—Persian, Egyptian, Assyrian, Babylonian— thought of man as a despised figure who groveled before deities and despots. The Greeks picked man up and set him on his feet. "The world is full of wonders," sang Sophocles, "but nothing is more wonderful than man." The Greeks depicted their gods in idealized human form, like the smiling Apollo shown on the opposite page. What the world 2,400 years later would think of the Greeks the Athenian statesman Pericles foretold *(above)* in his eloquent funeral oration on the first casualties of the Peloponnesian War. The picture essay beginning here combines the proud affirmations of Pericles with photographs of Greek masterpieces that sum up the everlasting Greek achievement.

THE SERENE SPIRIT OF GREECE *shines from this Apollo, god of the intellect. It was cast in bronze 2,400 years ago, lost some 400 years later and found again under a Piraeus street only in 1959.*

"*Our love of what is beautiful does not lead to extravagance*"

WORKADAY JUG, *turned out by endless thousands to carry wine and olive oil to all parts of the ancient world, still stands witness to the Greek love of beauty.*

To ARCHITECTURE, as well as to the handcrafting of house-hold utensils, classical Greece brought a great feeling for purity, elegance—and function. These qualities are clearly stated in the strong Doric columns, the austerely harmonious steps and the delicately symmetrical vase shown on these pages. An unexpected lecturer on these matters was the old soldier Xenophon, who, in his delightful book on household manage-ment, wrote: "It is beautiful to see the footgear ranged in a row . . . garments sorted according to their use . . . cooking pots ar-ranged with sense and symmetry." Beauty was above price. When the King of Bithynia offered to pay the debts of the im-poverished people of Cnidus if only they would sell him Praxite-les' statue of Aphrodite, they spurned him. But a taste for beauty must not be overindulged; the Greek rule that everything in life must be enjoyed in moderation applied even here. Socrates warned that "when a man allows music to play upon him and to pour into his soul through the funnel of his ears those sweet and soft and melancholy airs . . . he becomes a feeble warrior."

"*Where the rewards of valor*
are the greatest,
there you will find also the best
and bravest spirits among the people"

T HE GREEK regard for individual worth applied equally
in peace and war—so their fighting force was organized on democratic lines. Xenophon, taking command of 10,000 men, explained his plans to his army and then
said, "If anyone has a better plan to propose, let him do so."
Athens elected its generals. A man might walk to one war a
common soldier and ride to the next a general. War was considered the supreme test of a man—and not beneath the concern
of the gods. Aeschylus, writing his own epitaph, ignored enduring dramas and noted only the courage he displayed against
the Persians. Headlong bravery was the least that was expected
of Greek fighters. But style in war was particularly admired. The
Greeks esteemed Diëneces the Spartan who, told that the enemy
hosts at Thermopylae were so large their arrows would hide the
sun, replied, "So much the better, we shall fight in the shade."

WARRIOR GODS *march into combat against an enemy force composed of giants. This is*
part of a frieze at Delphi telling how immortal gods defeated mortals in a pitched battle.

"We are free and tolerant in our private lives;

but in public affairs we keep to the law. . . . We give our obedience

to those whom we put in positions of authority"

SELF-GOVERNMENT *is honored in a relief showing Democracy placing a wreath on the people of Athens. It was erected in the marketplace to remind the citizens to value their freedom.*

STATUE TO FREEDOM, *the famous Victory, was erected on the island of Samothrace, possibly to commemorate a naval victory by the Greeks against foes who would have enslaved them.*

D EMOCRATIC GOVERNMENT began as a Greek concept. The Greeks heeded law and prized order. But they also had a passion for freedom and abhorred corruption and tyranny. Aristophanes could denounce in a play an officeholder as "this public robber, this yawning gulf of plunder, this devouring Charybdis, this villain, this villain, this villain." And according to law: "If anyone rise up against the people with a view to tyranny . . . whoever kills him . . . shall be blameless." No male citizen was barred from office, and in Athens most served at some time because many positions were filled by lot.

"Our love of the things of the mind does not make us soft"

A MAN OF THE MIND, *Aristotle defined the state of happiness as the exercise of all a man's "vital powers along the lines of excellence."*

THE GREEKS gave equal respect to mental and physical prowess because they believed that the ideal life would be one spent in the pursuit of excellence in all things. The complete man would be equally active as an athlete, philosopher, judge, poet or at any other worthy pursuit. The philosopher Socrates once worked as an apprentice sculptor; the playwright Sophocles not only served as a general but was also at different times imperial treasurer, diplomat and priest. At athletic festivals prizes were also awarded for the best poets and the best rhapsodists, dancers and musicians.

MEN OF ACTION, *young riders easily keep their prancing horses under control. This frieze depicts the Panathenaic procession in honor of the goddess Athena that took place once every four years.*

"Mighty indeed are the marks and monuments...we have left"

THE JOCKEY, *urging on a horse that has long since fallen victim to the ravages of time, is a bronze that dates from the later period of Greek art. It shows a tenseness foreign to the classical period.*

SCULPTURE was the art form most favored by the Greeks, and for a logical reason. They made monuments to honor their gods, to commemorate victories, to record religious rites—but what they always depicted was man. Sculptors combined selected features to produce the idealized human figures that have been found from the westernmost Mediterranean to India. Over the centuries Greek art ranged from serene representations like the charioteer (*opposite*) to nervous, vital figures like the jockey (*above*). No matter what the mood, the works still testify to the Greek belief in the wonder of man.

THE DELPHI CHARIOTEER, *fashioned in bronze at the height of the classical period, illustrates restraint under pressure, a quality much sought after by the Greeks of ancient times.*

2

DARK AGE
AND NEW DAWN

The Greeks of historical times, which date from about 750 B.C., believed themselves to be descended from a legendary race of heroes. Men of prodigious physique and energy, these heroes sailed to the end of the world for a golden sheepskin, warred against the Trojans for 10 years over a beautiful woman, and one of them singlehandedly cleaned incredibly filthy stables in a day. For many centuries scholars assumed that these heroes and their adventures were pure fiction, but we now know that they had some basis in fact.

For nearly a century archeologists have been uncovering evidence of a rich civilization, centered at the city of Mycenae, that flourished between 1600 and 1200 B.C.—and Mycenae was the home of Agamemnon, the King who in legend led the Achaeans (the ancient name for the Greeks) into the Trojan War. This long-lost Mycenaean world was originally a development of a still older world, the brilliant Minoan civilization of Crete which dominated the Aegean from about 1600 to 1400 B.C. The Minoans were a lively, pleasure-loving and sensuous people—fond of bright colors, intricate games (they played a version of backgammon) and elegant clothes. Their homes, sometimes five stories high, had light-wells and setback terraces. Their palaces contained a system of plumbing (they even had flush toilets) unmatched for sanitary nicety until Victorian times. Some of their engineering skills, if not all their cultural refinements, were taken over by their Mycenaean heirs.

The Mycenaeans themselves were spectacular builders. Their palaces were built within formidable citadels with walls 10 feet thick, and some of their royal tombs were enormous beehive structures made of stones weighing, sometimes, as much as 120 tons. They were also immensely wealthy, especially in metals, and most especially in gold. In Mycenaean tombs, diggers have found death masks and breastplates of gold; bronze swords and daggers; gold and silver drinking cups; gold rings and diadems; and thin sheets of gold used as funeral wrappings for the bodies of two small royal children. The tombs also disclose something of the physical characteristics of these people. They were taller and broader-faced than the Minoans; the men were mustachioed and sometimes bearded.

NOBLE LADIES OF MYCENAEAN GREECE *set out in a chariot to attend a hunt. Their era, 13 centuries before Christ, gloried in mighty deeds of war and hunting and adorned its palaces with pictures of expeditions like this one.*

One corpse had apparently suffered from gallstones —a diagnosis which suggests a rich diet—and another had a fractured skull which had been neatly trepanned—thus giving us the earliest record of this surgical operation in Europe.

Decisions of a Mycenaean king and his court were carried out by an officialdom consisting, in diminishing order, of military leaders, administrative officials, charioteers and mayors of the group of villages that surrounded the city. Archeologists have discovered the actual records, kept by this efficient bureaucracy, of tax assessments, land holdings, agricultural stores, and inventories of slaves, horses, chariots and chariot parts ("one pair wheels bound with silver, one pair wheels bound with bronze, unfit for service").

These records, inscribed on clay tablets in a script (called Linear B by scholars) only recently deciphered, also list more than 100 Mycenaean occupations. Among them are goldsmiths, shipwrights, masons, bakers, cooks, woodcutters, messengers, longshoremen, oarsmen, saddlers, shepherds, dry cleaners, doctors, heralds, potters, foresters, carpenters, bowmakers, weavers, bath attendants and unguent boilers.

In sum, the Mycenaeans were an accomplished and enterprising people, worthy successors to the Minoans. But they were unlike the peaceful Minoans in one important aspect: a principal Mycenaean business seems to have been war—or, to put it more baldly, brigandage and piracy. Military enterprises took the Mycenaeans far from home on adventurous missions 1,300 years before the birth of Christ. According to Hittite records—the Hittites controlled a powerful empire in Asia Minor from a stronghold east of present-day Ankara—marauding bands of Achaeans were harassing the coast of Asia Minor in the middle of the 13th Century B.C. On one long-drawn-out expedition they laid siege to the city of Troy in the war which legend said was fought for the stolen princess, Helen, and lasted 10 years.

And then, less than a century later, this vigorous, splendid civilization came to a terrible end. It was obliterated by successive invasions of far less civilized Greeks from the north, called Dorians. For 450 years, between 1200 and 750 B.C., the Greek world passed through a Dark Age from which survived only scattered legends and some unrewarding artifacts.

The Dorians attacked and destroyed Mycenaean cities when they were weakened by war. The conquerors lived as squatters in burned-out Mycenaean palaces but did not rebuild them. Record-keeping vanished, the art of writing disappeared. Handicrafts decayed at lamentable speed. Finely worked arms in bronze were replaced by crude (but more effective) weapons made of iron; burial in magnificent tombs was largely superseded by perfunctory cremation.

The tightly organized Mycenaean society was totally disintegrated by the Dorian assault. Many of the Mycenaeans became dispossessed, purposeless wanderers. To this chaos of moving people was added the movement of the conquerors themselves, but their travels were purposeful. Not content with ravaging the Mycenaean cities, the Dorians pressed southward and seized the Laconian plain. From the Greek mainland they sailed across the Mediterranean to Crete, subjugating it completely. And from Crete it was only a short voyage to Rhodes and its neighboring islands, which suffered a similar fate.

This was the Dark Age of Greece. Although a few remnants of the old Mycenaean culture remained here and there—on the island of Cyprus; in the mountains of Arcadia; and in Attica, clustered around the small town of Athens—most of the old Achaean world fell apart. People lost their old stability and order. They lived as best they could. Brother was pitted against brother, children against parents, friend against friend. One of Greece's ear-

A TIME OF CRUMBLING EMPIRES

Pharaoh Ramses III, depicted on a stone pylon at a Nile temple, is seen repelling Egypt's attackers early in the 12th Century B.C. This period, when Dorian invaders were overrunning Greece, was elsewhere marked by the eclipse of great empires. Egypt, despite Ramses' victories, slowly lost its mastery in the Mediterranean, and the Hittites were overthrown in Asia Minor. Among the numerous small nations to rise and flourish in the power vacuum were Phoenicia, whose aggressive traders colonized Carthage, and the Hebrew kingdom, which reached its apogee in the reigns of David and Solomon from 1005 to 925 B.C. India remained a checkerboard of warring city states through an era that produced its vast epic poems, the *Mahabharata* and the *Ramayana*. Until the fierce warriors of Assyria reached the peak of their power in the Eighth Century B.C., China under the Chou Dynasty was the only extensive empire in the ancient world.

liest and best-known poets, Hesiod, lived at the very close of this period and described it in detail with the hope that he could induce the Greeks to change their ways. To Hesiod the Mycenaean age embodied all that was beautiful and good. His own time was full of violence and brutality, intolerance and indifference, stealing, cheating, lying:

> No brother will claim from brother the love
>   once claimed,
> And parents will quickly age, dishonored
>   and shamed,
> And men will scorn them and bitter words
>   they'll say,
> Hard-hearted, no longer god-fearing. They'll
>   not repay
> The cost of their nurture, but might their
>   right they'll call;
> And ravaging men will break through a city
>   wall.

In the first centuries after the fall of the Mycenaean civilization, each city, with its surrounding hamlets and farms, became a separate social unit. Borders shifted constantly, and what little order existed was usually military in origin: the city was in effect a garrison governed by a commander and his captains. Gradually borders became fixed along natural boundary lines, and if the lines were defensible, the city and its surrounding countryside survived to become an independent community, a city-state. Military governments became hereditary monarchies. Kings ruled by divine right and were considered to be descended from gods. A king was the religious leader of his community as well as its secular head. Nowhere in Greece, however, did kings claim actually to be gods, as some Asian kings did. Nor did they demand the abject obedience or absolute authority that Oriental rulers claimed as their right.

Along with a developing sense of civic independence, the Greeks began to acquire certain uniform cultural patterns that transcended local boundaries and local styles in dress, decoration and speech. They became willing to learn from one another, to change their ideas and their ways of doing things. Sometimes they shared technical skills, sometimes tastes. The Greeks' own name for themselves, Hellenes, originated in the Dark Age. Greek pottery began to take on a distinctively Hellenic character, despite regional variations. And they shared a common language, so that despite their different dialects they were intelligible to one another. From these tentative beginnings sprang the main features that were eventually to define Hellenic civilization—the intellectual and political freedom, the sense of cultural unity.

Not all of Greece reacted in the same fashion to the Dorian onslaught or survived the subsequent Dark Age in the same manner. The early history of two of the most influential city-states was of great moment. Strangely, at the outset, the first was not very important and the other may not even have existed in Mycenaean times. Nevertheless, what happened to Athens and Sparta in the Dark Age set the stage for the roles they were to play in the later Golden Age of Greece—and paradoxically insured the end of that great Age. Sparta, settled by the Dorians on the site of what may have been a tiny village, was destined to remain essentially Dorian in outlook thereafter. Athens held off the Dorians and was able to give refuge to fellow Mycenaeans fleeing the invaders. In the crowded city were preserved elements of the splendid past on which a glorious future would some day be built.

Centuries later Athens and Sparta represented opposing philosophies in Greek life—intellectual and political freedom against stern, military discipline. When the Dorians settled at Sparta they organized it as a military camp. It kept that character until they had subdued the neighboring settlements in the Laconian plain. Then, for a period of time, Sparta became one of the brightest centers of the culture that flowered at the close of the Dark Age. It produced exquisite pottery, and was noted for its festivals of song and dance. But when military concerns again became uppermost, these disappeared, and Sparta, by this time a major Greek city-state, reverted to its earlier attitudes. Its citizens became pawns of the state, rigidly controlled from birth to death. From seven onward its children were trained for war, learning not only to use weapons but to endure physical hardship and accept discipline without question. Home life was practically non-existent. The men ate at a common mess, could not marry before the age of 20, and could not live with their wives (except surreptitiously) until the age of 30. After 30 they were permitted to have a household, but their children belonged to the state. Even during periods when the state was in no immediate danger, Sparta remained conservative and austere in outlook, and made a virtue of extreme simplicity.

Athens was able to fight off the Dorian invaders because it was on a natural fortress, the rocky Acropolis. Then refugees from the other Mycenaean cities, among them the royal family of Pylos, flocked to Athens and the surrounding countryside of Attica. Soon the population grew too large for the comparatively limited space available. But Attica had several superb harbors, among them Piraeus, only five miles from Athens, and in about 1100 B.C., emigration began. Greeks sailed out into the Aegean to find new homes on the Aegean islands and on the western coast of Asia Minor. These émigré colonies of Greeks in and around the Aegean came to be called Ionia.

The first of the Ionian colonies were on the islands of Naxos, Chios and Samos, but others soon followed on the mainland. The soil was rich, the coastline well provided with harbors, and rivers like the winding Maeander offered passage inland for trade and expansion. The Greek colonists were not always welcomed by the native population, and so the newcomers fortified themselves in walled towns. Eventually these precautions stood them in good stead, for as the colonies prospered they were menaced by the Cimmerians and the Lydians, who had, one after the other, supplanted the Hittites in Asia Minor. Despite these harassments the Ionians were much better off than their countrymen at home. If they could not hope to re-create the old Mycenaean world, they were at least free to fashion a new one.

Like all expatriates the Ionians were extremely conscious of their ties with the homeland. Their leaders included princes of ancient Mycenaean lineage, and they spoke a modified form of the dialect spoken in Attica. They kept the gods and ceremonies and social systems that they had brought with them. Their houses were built on the traditional Greek plan—one room surrounding a central hearth —and their pottery, elegantly decorated with geometric patterns, was copied from the pottery made in Athens. Most important of all, the Ionians preserved the epic songs and stories that had been passed down from Greek antiquity.

The epics were crucial to Greek civilization. Not only were they the chief relaxation for the Greeks in the early period, but they also performed for pre-literate Greeks a number of functions that were essential to their survival. Later, they were to live on as a strong element in the art and literature of the Western world. For these reasons it is appropriate to stop here to examine in some detail the nature of the Greek epics and to discuss the greatest of the bards who composed them—Homer.

To the Greeks, struggling to regain a lost glory, the epic songs were entertainment, inspiring history, reminders of a time when to be a Greek was

to be strong and brave and noble and capable of prodigious achievements. They were also lessons in noble and ignoble conduct, and repositories of tales on the ways of the gods. Thus the bard imparted instruction while he gave delight. The legends themselves were only a framework to which he added extemporaneous elaboration, designed to fit the needs and temper of a specific audience. Over the years, succeeding generations of bards evolved a technique which depended heavily on a very large number of standardized forms. There was, first of all, an established outline for each legend and a cast of characters whose names and personalities were always much the same. There were also set descriptions for certain recurring places and events, including conventionalized figures of speech. Bards used a huge stock of phrases that fell automatically into verse: "wine-dark sea," "long-shadowing spear," "death that lays at length," "rosy-fingered dawn," "brazen sky," "windy Troy."

The epic drew upon several kinds of legends or myths: some concerned with gods, others with gods and men, and others with men alone. In the Dark Age, when bards first began to perfect them, myths offered a way of answering hard questions about human nature and the universe for audiences unable to consider these matters scientifically. The myths made abstract ideas comprehensible by presenting the ideas as they affected real people caught in recognizable events.

The myths concerned with gods were intended primarily to explain religious matters, such as the changes that occurred when one set of gods was displaced by another. The substitution of the Greek gods on Mount Olympus for the old Minoan gods is explained, for instance, by the myth which tells of the brutal struggle between Zeus, ruler of the Olympian gods, and his father Cronos; Zeus finally overcomes his father and throws him into Tartarus, the ancient Hell.

GREEK ALPHABET LETTER	Α	Β	Γ	Δ	Ε	Ζ	Η	Θ	Ι
NAME OF LETTER	alpha	beta	gamma	delta	epsilon	zeta	eta	theta	iota
ENGLISH TRANSLITERATION	a	b	g	d	e	z	e	th	i

The myths of the gods also dealt with many matters other than those directly concerned with the gods' personal genealogies. Sometimes they explained how and why the gods controlled nature. The changing seasons are accounted for in the myth of Hades, god of the underworld, who falls in love with Persephone, the daughter of the earth goddess Demeter, and carries her off to his kingdom. While Demeter grieves, no crops grow, whereupon other gods intercede with Hades, who finally agrees to let Persephone leave the underworld and spend part of the year with her mother.

In other myths, human actions are explained. The Oedipus legend concerns a phenomenon familiar to us, the unconscious desire of a boy to supplant his father in his mother's affections. And many myths about gods and men also point a moral: Bellerophon acquires a winged horse with the help of the gods, and in his pride tries to fly on it up to Mount Olympus. For this presumptuousness he is thrown off and lamed, and wanders alone for the rest of his days. Tantalus, greatly favored of the gods, is made to suffer eternal hunger and thirst because at a dinner for them he served the flesh of his own son.

Still other myths about men are really embellished versions of history. They are full of action and crisis, violence and suffering, and are amazingly varied in theme. The Greeks refused to shrink from any subject, no matter how fearful or horrible, and they cared little for happy endings, preferring instead to hear of courageous men who are doomed to be overcome by catastrophe. Very likely these tastes were molded by the hard conditions of their own lives. Among these doomed mortals is Agamemnon, the conqueror of Troy, who is killed by his wife Clytaemnestra, who in her turn is killed by their son Orestes. Heracles, most prodigious of heroes, kills his wife and sons in a fit of madness, and later dies himself in torment. Ajax, a leading

THE GREEK ALPHABET, *adapted from Phoenician script during the Eighth Century B.C., took on several local forms as it spread through early Greece. One version, the Chalcidian alphabet of western Greece, appears at upper left, scratched on a rooster-shaped vase of the Seventh Century B.C. Another, the East Ionic alphabet, became standard throughout Greece after Athens adopted it officially at the end of the Fifth Century B.C. The Greek letters, seven of which were the first characters ever to represent true vowel sounds independently, were adapted by the Romans and passed from their Latin into the English alphabet. About 12 per cent of the words in the English language are directly derived from Greek roots. A sampling of Greek words, with their English derivatives, appears in the box below.*

GREEK WORDS (English Transliteration)	ANCIENT GREEK MEANING	ENGLISH DERIVATIVE
ΑΚΑΔΗΜΙΑ (akademeia)	The Academy	Academy
ΒΑΡΒΑΡΟΣ (barbaros)	Barbarian, foreigner	Barbarian
ΒΛΑΣΦΗΜΙΑ (blasphemia)	Profanity, slander	Blasphemy
ΧΑΡΑΚΤΗΡ (charakter)	A brand, stamp, mark	Character
ΚΡΙΤΙΚΟΣ (kritikos)	Discerning	Critic
ΔΕΣΠΟΤΗΣ (despotes)	Master	Despot
ΔΥΝΑΜΙΚΟΣ (dynamikos)	Powerful	Dynamic
ΥΓΙΕΙΝΗ (hygieine)	Hygiene	Hygiene
ΟΣΤΡΑΚΙΣΜΟΣ (ostrakismos)	Ostracism	Ostracism
ΠΟΙΗΤΗΣ (poietes)	Creator, poet	Poet
ΠΡΑΚΤΙΚΗ (praktike)	Business, practical knowledge	Practical
ΣΤΩΙΚΟΣ (stoikos)	Stoic, philosopher	Stoic
ΣΧΟΛΗ (schole)	Free time, leisure, discussion	School
ΤΥΡΑΝΝΟΣ (tyrannos)	Tyrant, dictator	Tyrant

Κ	Λ	Μ	Ν	Ξ	Ο	Π	Ρ	Σ	Τ	Υ	Φ	Χ	Ψ	Ω
kappa	lambda	mu	nu	xi	omicron	pi	rho	sigma	tau	upsilon	phi	chi	psi	omega
c, k	l	m	n	x	o	p	r, rh	s	t	y, u	ph	ch	ps	o

warrior in the siege of Troy, goes mad because he is not awarded Achilles' armor when Achilles dies, then kills himself in shame over his behavior.

The myths also contain touches of fellow feeling and even of romance: Perseus rescues Andromeda from a sea monster at the end of the world; Alcestis offers to die in place of her husband, Admetus, when his span of life runs out, and Admetus, accepting her offer, does so tearfully and gives her a magnificent funeral. Most myths are full of anecdotal detours that are replete with bits of traditional lore that have little or nothing to do with the main message, but are nevertheless important adjuncts to that message. Like all folk tales, these anecdotes had an immediate appeal, and helped to keep the audience attentive and receptive. But unlike much folk wisdom, which is distilled into animal stories, the Greek version is found chiefly in stories of men. Such tales were closer to them and more relevant to their problems. And they fitted nicely into the careers of wandering heroes such as Odysseus, whose stories were a long series of adventures.

The climax of this creative tradition in legend and song came in the latter part of the Eighth Century B.C. in the person of Homer and his two great epic poems, the *Iliad* and the *Odyssey*. Little is known of Homer himself—he is thought to have lived either at Smyrna or on the island of Chios—but his two masterpieces mark the dawn of European literature. The old Dark Age epics provided Homer with story material and a metric form which subsequently became the meter for all Greek epic poetry—the dactylic hexameter. Twenty-six centuries later the British poet Alfred Lord Tennyson called this meter "the stateliest measure ever molded by the lips of man," but the rhythms of ancient Greek came not from variations in beat, but variations in the length of syllables—so that Greek dactylic hexameter cannot truly be translated into English. The closest English equivalent is the meter used in Longfellow's poem, *Evangeline*.

But the Homeric poems are far more than magnificent poetry. The *Iliad* and *Odyssey* became the source books of Greek religion, and Homer was considered by later Greeks to be the founder of their history, philosophy, drama, poetry and science. His themes were an endless source of inspiration to Greek artists and orators. And for us today he is a fascinating source of information on the Greek world as it was in his lifetime, and the world as he thought it to be in Mycenaean days.

Although he drew upon the myths that had come down to him through the centuries, Homer added much that was his own. His treatment of the main theme of both poems, as well as their individual episodes, is far more sensitive and perceptive. He took the primitive tales of monsters and cannibals and desperate risks and enlivened them with a generous and tender vision of life. In earlier versions of the tale, Achilles was no doubt a prodigious warrior who killed his enemy Hector and then mutilated his body as a sign of triumph. But Homer's Achilles is moved to give the dead body to Hector's father Priam. Similarly, there are many old tales of a wanderer who is cast up from the sea and saved by a princess whom he marries. Homer's wanderer, Odysseus, is also rescued by a charming princess, Nausicaa, but does not marry her. Odysseus has a wife at home and so, instead of marriage, a touching friendship develops between the battered seaman and the young girl.

All of Homer's characters, even those to whom he pays little attention—swineherds, ordinary soldiers, serving women, worthless suitors for the hand of a rich lady—are real and convincing people. Each episode abounds in the endless variety of human conduct. Homer himself never obtrudes, hardly ever passes judgment. Everything that he has to say is said through the words and actions of his characters. His patrons probably wanted no more than tales of heroism, but he gave them a whole view of the world, of the gods at their appointed tasks, of men and women pursuing their destinies, of every mood from grim vengeance to uproarious farce, of palaces and gardens, remote islands and rocky shores. Behind every story his imagination is at work, seeing humans as they really are, understanding why they act as they do, portraying them with insight even when they are bad, and when they are good, with warmth and gentle affection.

Homer was the culmination of the new spirit that flowered in Ionia, but he was not the only manifestation of that spirit. In the plastic arts, potters, metalsmiths and woodcarvers moved in new directions. Figurines in clay and bronze began to hint at the body in movement: the draperies were still stylized, but there was a body underneath. Temples were adorned with wooden sculptures, and as Greek sailors and merchants ventured farther afield, they brought home jewelry and trinkets of gold and carved ivory.

Soon the Greek homeland began to copy and compete with its Ionian colonies. Although the city-states still kept their petty kings and autonomous governments, the people themselves mingled freely and easily, living busy lives and tempering their activity with communal religious rites. One of the earliest of these was the festival of song, dance and games on the island of Delos, in honor of Apollo. A far more famous event was the great games held at Olympia every four years to honor Zeus. All Greece participated in the Olympian games. Each city sent its best athletes to compete in wrestling, foot racing, boxing, leaping, discus throwing, javelin hurling and chariot racing, and each man gave of his best to honor himself, his city and his gods. To the Greek people the games were one more case of their shared culture.

One final development at the close of the Dark Age made Greek unity even stronger: the appearance of a Greek alphabet. Writing had existed in Mycenaean times, but it was a clumsy tool, good enough for making lists and for bookkeeping but ill fitted for literature. The new alphabet was based on that of Phoenicia, but it acquired vowels to supplement the Phoenician consonants. Admirably adapted to many needs, it spread rapidly to all parts of the Greek world. One of the earliest examples of its use is a verse about love incised on a drinking cup found at Ischia, an island at the entrance to the Bay of Naples:

I am Nestor's cup.
He who would drink from this cup
Shall be assailed by the subtle seductive
Persuasion of beautifully crowned Aphrodite.

With an alphabet, many matters which were previously entrusted to memory or limited to itemized record-keeping could be written down as literary documents. Laws were incised on stone and set up in the public square for all the people to read, and Homer's poetry was probably set down in writing within his own lifetime. Writing made it possible to conduct trade negotiations much more efficiently and provided a much more effective means of recording history.

The Greek alphabet took several forms, one of them leading to the Etruscan alphabet, which in turn inspired the Roman alphabet that the Western world uses today. But despite minor variations, it remained essentially the same down through its long career, a fine and flexible instrument. With writing and literature, and a promising renaissance in arts and crafts, Ionia emerged from the Dark Age into the sunlight of Hellenism and began to spread its message of beauty and refinement throughout the Greek world.

IN GENERAL COMBAT *helmeted warriors fight at Troy, where, Homer reported, "showers of big stones battered the shields of the fighting men. . . ."*

OF WAR AND A WANDERER

The picture above and most of the other photographs in this essay are taken from a frieze in grayish pock-marked sandstone stored in the Kunsthistorisches Museum in Vienna. The frieze, dating from the early Fourth Century B.C., was discovered a century ago on the walls of a tomb in Gjölbaschi, on modern-day Turkey's Mediterranean coast. Because it is too large for convenient display—its two superimposed rows of low-relief carvings total 600 feet in length—it is shown only on request, and it has rarely been photographed and even more rarely published. It is the most monumental attempt to depict the mighty deeds of the warriors who fought at the siege of Troy, ancient Ilion that Homer sings of in the *Iliad.* Its many panels also contain a scene of the homecoming of Odysseus which Homer recounts in the *Odyssey.* Heightening the spell that Homer's poems still weave, these stories in stone give visual form to major episodes from the two epics.

TROJAN TROOPS ON GUARD *stand atop the walls of their city. Twice in the course of frenzied struggles, Greek warriors reached the walls, only to be frustrated by the gods, who said it was not time for Troy to fall.*

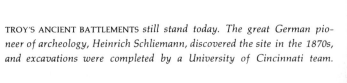

TROY'S ANCIENT BATTLEMENTS *still stand today. The great German pioneer of archeology, Heinrich Schliemann, discovered the site in the 1870s, and excavations were completed by a University of Cincinnati team.*

THE CLANGOROUS SIEGE OF A PROUD CITY

The fighting around Troy's walls lasted for 10 grinding years. The *Iliad's* time span is scarcely six weeks of the last year of that war. But this poem is an exciting story, ringing with the clash of armored and embattled men. For the Greeks who first heard it, it expressed the heroic ideals of their own aristocratic era, freshly emerged from the Dark Age, and served as a religious document that set the characters of the Olympian family. For all time it is high tragedy—the story of a great man brought low by his pride and anger. Achilles, the Greek warrior who was incomparable in battle, is the central figure of this poem. After a heated quarrel with Agamemnon, Achilles, furiously angry, sulks in his tent while the Trojans under Hector, son of Troy's King Priam, drive the Greeks away from Troy's walls. But when his dearest friend, Patroclus, is killed, Achilles comes forth to lead the invaders back to Troy. There he slays Hector. A funeral is held for Patroclus. Then the sorrowing Achilles, moved to compassion by the mediation of the gods, gives Hector's body to Priam, to be buried as befits a fallen hero.

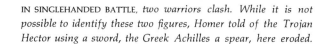

IN SINGLEHANDED BATTLE, *two warriors clash. While it is not possible to identify these two figures, Homer told of the Trojan Hector using a sword, the Greek Achilles a spear, here eroded.*

MAN-TO-MAN COMBAT OF GREAT WARRIORS

Armies maneuver and fight in the *Iliad*. But heroes —the men whose bravery gives added dignity to all mankind—are proved in individual combat: Hector against Patroclus, Achilles against Hector. Homer seldom speaks of ordinary soldiers; his attention is focused on heroic figures, often on the losers. The Greeks thought victory glorious and a defeat heroically endured only a shade less glorious. The real goal was not victory, but fame. A man could accept death, but he would so die that the living would remember. Achilles, sorrowing over Patroclus' death, vows to win fame for himself by avenging his friend. "Now may I win a glorious name!" he cries. "May they know that I have been long away from the battle! May I bring sobs and groaning to some wives of Troy and Dardania." And Hector, knowing he will die at Greek hands, takes comfort in the judgment of posterity. "Then men will say in far distant generations to come, as they sail along the shore, 'Yonder is the barrow of a man dead long ago, a champion whom famous Hector slew.' So my fame will never be forgotten."

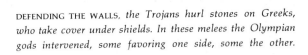

A MOMENT OF DESTINY *comes for one soldier as another grasps him by the hair and prepares to stab him. The Greeks thought Zeus at such a moment weighed a man's fate on scales.*

A ROLE FOR THE GODS

The war began when three goddesses—Hera, Athena and Aphrodite—quarreled over which was the fairest. A beauty contest was set with Paris of Troy as judge. All three goddesses tried to bribe him, but Aphrodite won by promising him the most beautiful wife in the world. This promise obliged her to help Paris carry off the lovely Helen, wife of King Menelaus of Sparta. As the Greeks sailed against Troy to recover Helen, the other gods took sides. Zeus, chief of the gods, tried to keep his bickering family out of the battle, but his wife Hera, who favored the Greeks, put on her most subtle perfumes and lulled Zeus to sleep. When next Zeus looked at the battlefield the Trojans had suffered heavy losses.

POSEIDON'S PERCH *is Mount Phengari, the highest point on Samothrace, where he watched over Greek ships. When the Trojans threatened, he rode his golden chariot to the rescue.*

FLEEING THE CITY *a Trojan wife (left) rides off after her husband. Most men still in the city at its capture were slaughtered, the city was razed, and women and children enslaved.*

BACK AT HOME, *Odysseus, disguised as an old beggar (below), and his son enter the banquet hall of his own house, where wily suitors for his wife's hand have long been ensconced.*

AN EXCITING TALE OF DARING DEEDS

The Greeks won their war with a famous ruse that military men and statesmen often try to repeat in other ways. They gave Troy a gift—a wooden horse with Greeks hidden inside. While the Trojans slept, the Greeks crept out and opened the city's gates to the rest of their army. Masters at last, the Greek soldiers saw Helen reunited with Menelaus, and everyone started for home. But one among them, the ingenious Odysseus who had devised the wooden horse trick, found the route 10 years long. Homer tells of his experiences in his second great poem, the *Odyssey*, a rousing story of adventure. Odysseus reached the land of the Lotus Eaters, then got trapped in the cave of the Cyclops. Afterward, he had troubles with the enchantress Circe who first playfully turned his men into swine, then sent Odysseus to the gates of Hades, where he chatted with some old war comrades. But he finally got home in time to kill the men who had been eating up his stores while courting his presumed widow, the faithful Penelope.

3

A CONFIDENT ARISTOCRACY

After the appearance of the Greek alphabet, sometime during the Eighth Century B.C., the Greeks at last begin to speak to us in their own contemporary words. The evidence, after so long a time, is naturally fragmentary and haphazard but its lively, significant details add to our knowledge in many areas.

The Greek economic revival, marked by a resurgence of fine craftsmanship and an expansion of foreign trade, soon introduced a fundamental change in the structure of Greek life. In almost every state except Sparta and Thessaly the petty kings of tradition were deposed or reduced to figureheads. Sparta, with its rigid conservatism, perpetuated its ancient dual monarchy, and Thessaly, with its agrarian society of widely separated landholders, kept its system of hereditary kings until the Fifth Century B.C. Elsewhere, kings were removed from office for good reason—abuse of power—even though, as sole repository of custom and law, they had not been bound to conform to any code.

Where the kings were deprived of their power, authority passed to the local aristocracy. Thus the great step forward was made from government by a single ruler to government by a group of men. The new rulers were the descendants of the warriors who had seized land and established estates during the Dark Age. Initially only landowners could be aristocrats; later some wealthy merchants and manufacturers were admitted to the class. They were men of leisure, active in sports and outdoor pursuits, if only as part of their military training. They were accustomed to country life, but not afraid to put to sea. They were versed in the social skills demanded by life in a small community. Taught from childhood to take part in singing and dancing, they shared a common interest in music and the art of the spoken and sung word. And they subscribed to a strict code of conduct that required them to be truthful, trustworthy, courteous (even to enemies), courageous, respectful of the rights of others, generous with their possessions (as far as their means would permit), immune to the temptation to cheat, and proud of the code itself.

These aristocrats may have lacked the superabundant vitality of later Greeks, but they never-

A RUIN AT DELPHI *magnificently evokes the search for splendor at the holy site. Built by the architect Theodorus of Phocaea, this was a tholos, or round building, but what it was designed for has been lost to history.*

theless had a splendid energy. They excelled in many graces, but were not in the least effete. Unlike members of some aristocracies, they did not enjoy a position secure enough to allow them to become overrefined.

The political and geographical center of Greek life was the *polis*, or city-state. The *polis* came to mean, and to be, much more than merely the seat of government. It included the lands around it, and was the meeting-place of people who lived inside and outside its walls. In it business was transacted, manufacturing was carried on, ceremonies and rites were conducted, public affairs discussed and decided on. Although the number of people who actually lived within the walls of the *polis* was small, its total population included townsmen and countrymen, and in maritime centers like Corinth and Athens, seafaring men as well. Farmers, craftsmen, tradesmen and sailors mingled freely. Life was at once varied and intimate, full of various kinds of civic activity, including that one to which the term "politics" now refers.

The aristocrats who governed the *polis* regarded themselves as superior beings, and associated mainly with their own class. They believed themselves specially qualified by birth and breeding for the task of looking after public affairs—and since it was to their own advantage to keep the city secure and prosperous, they often showed great talent in doing so. Nevertheless, there were repeated clashes of interest between the aristocrats and the common people. Finally the commoners demanded and got a written code of laws. The earliest of these codes date from the Seventh Century B.C., before the word "democracy" existed. They dealt mainly with homicide, which had hitherto been settled by family feud, and with property ownership. They also dealt with contracts between two persons, and they laid down rules for the appointment of magistrates and other officials. Sometimes they even regulated

the form of government. One of these codes, prepared for Athens by a man named Draco in 621 B.C., was so harsh that "Draconian" became a synonym for extreme severity or cruelty in any area. Draco made the minor offense of cabbage-stealing punishable by death, and gave a creditor the right to the person of his debtor—in effect enslaving the debtor. But Draco's code also introduced the idea of justifiable homicide, and made a distinction between premeditated and involuntary manslaughter.

Under the aristocrats the *polis* acquired a more stable system of government and the rich civic life that came to differentiate the Greeks from their foreign neighbors. Long after the aristocrats had lost their power, the *polis* remained the focus of Greek life because of its inspired view of what a man's existence ought to be. Because their superiority supposedly came from the favor of the gods, the aristocrats considered that they were "good" men. But for them "good" was by no means an exclusively or even predominantly ethical concept. Goodness, or *aretē*, was an intrinsic excellence that existed in all things. A good man, the poet Simonides wrote, was "truly noble, in hands and feet and mind, fashioned foursquare without blemish."

According to this ideal of manhood, public honor and private honor were intimately related. A man owed it to himself to display his best qualities and be recognized for them, and the praise he received for his actions was a mark of his success. But success was not only a personal reward: it was an obligation he owed his city. If a man died for his city's honor, he was a "good" man. And during his lifetime he was expected to keep its laws, do nothing to disgrace it, maintain a certain sobriety of behavior among his fellows, and be worthy of his ancestry and his upbringing. In this view of "goodness," what are now considered strictly moral virtues were less important than the social ones, and mattered only when moral failure brought shame upon a man and his class. The aristocratic ideal of manhood was wide and generous. It did not restrict "goodness" to a specific field of behavior, but simply expected a man to be in every sense a man.

When civic and personal honor were this closely connected, an affront to one was an affront to the other. The city's interests were identified with personal interests. This helps to explain the Greek propensity for war. Although men went to war initially because their cities' reputations were at stake, they also did so for personal gain and for personal satisfaction. The fighting was essentially hand-to-hand, taxing a man to his utmost, physically and mentally. Thus war gave a man an opportunity to display those qualities most admired by his fellows. His prowess not only gained him their admiration but also brought honor to his city and was in equal measure a source of pride to himself and his family. Some idea of the intensity of this public pridefulness can be gotten from an epitaph on a stone slab in a tomb, dating from about 600 B.C., found on the island of Corcyra. It honors the courage in battle of a warrior felled by Ares, the god of war:

> This is the tomb of Arniadas. Him flashing-eyed Ares destroyed as he fought by the ships at the streams of Aratthus, displaying the highest valor amid the groans and shouts of war.

To die in battle was regarded as a fitting end to life, the right way to defy life's brevity. And when a Greek died in the defense of his city's honor, his name gained even greater dignity. He was mourned by his fellowmen, commemorated by a public memorial and thenceforth held in the highest esteem. Greeks in general thought only vaguely about life after death, and most men seemed doubt-ful that any existed. It was not for any hope of heaven that they died so willingly in battle, but rather because death in this form was ennobling in itself.

Although wars were ostensibly fought on points of civic honor, they also had economic causes. One of the most persistent of the latter was the perennial and insoluble difficulty created by a shortage of land. In times of peace and prosperity, when the population increased, this problem became acute. Often, there was not enough food simply because the available land was already being worked for all it could yield. And at best the Greek diet was by no means lavish. Then as now the staple foods were olive oil, fish, goat cheese, wine and bread. Goats and sheep provided occasional meat, as well as milk for cheese; and bees provided honey for sweetening. There were also nuts and figs, as delicacies. But otherwise the staples were rounded out with such homely items as beans, peas, cabbage, lettuce, lentils and garlic.

A possible solution to the need for more land was, of course, to seize a neighbor's. But this was not very satisfactory. Whole populations might be reduced to slavery, as the Spartans reduced their Messenian neighbors, but they could not be wholly obliterated—their labor was needed to farm the seized lands. And so they had to be fed. Because war did not solve the problem of land and food, the Greeks attempted an alternative. Capitalizing on their experience as seamen and their knowledge of trade, they organized parties of colonists and sent them abroad to settle in distant lands. This relieved the drain on the Greek food supply, and also provided the homeland with new sources for the produce and raw materials Greece lacked. The process, begun in the Eighth Century B.C., continued unabated for two centuries.

Greek colonization followed two main directions, north and west. To the north, colonies were planted first along the northern Aegean littoral, then on the shores of the Propontis (now the Sea of Marmara), and finally on the Crimean shore of the Black Sea. To the west the Greeks went into Sicily and southern Italy around 750 B.C., going up the western coast of Italy as far as the Bay of Naples. In about 600 B.C., Ionian Greeks from the city of Phocaea in Asia Minor, seeing the advantages of the natural harbor at present-day Marseilles, founded a settlement there called Massilia. East of Massilia, along the coast now famous as the French Riviera, ancient Greek settlements were established at Nicaea, Heracles Monoecus and Antipolis—present-day Nice, Monaco and Antibes. Massilia conducted a flourishing trade, bartering Greek manufactured products for Celtic raw materials. Their business took them up the Rhône River to the inland regions of Gaul and as far west as Cornwall and Ireland. One proof of this exchange is a large bronze vessel, found at Vix, near Châtillon-sur-Seine, about 140 miles southeast of Paris. It is a famous and beautiful example of archaic Greek craftsmanship, and must have been ordered by some local king for a high occasion, perhaps a wedding or a funeral.

Compared to the Greeks' achievements in other, less tangible fields, their talent for colonizing might seem relatively unimportant. And yet the Greek colonies were one of the most powerful means of spreading Greek civilization to other lands, though that was not their intention, and though the results only became visible with the passage of time.

Greek wares passing up the western coast of Italy reached the region of the Etruscans in central Italy when that fascinating civilization was at its height. The origins of the Etruscans are a mystery, and their language is scarcely understood, but it is evident that they fell under the enchantment of the Greek arts and modeled much of their own refined sculpture and ceramics on Greek examples.

Far to the east in the Crimea, Greek colonists

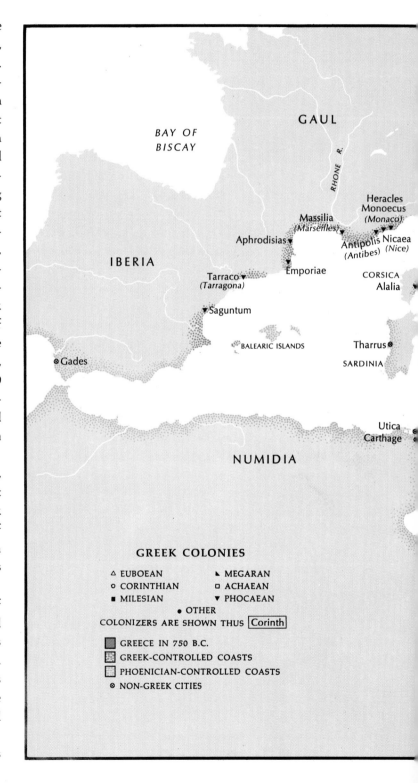

GREEK COLONIES

△ EUBOEAN   ◣ MEGARAN
○ CORINTHIAN   □ ACHAEAN
■ MILESIAN   ▼ PHOCAEAN
           ● OTHER
COLONIZERS ARE SHOWN THUS [Corinth]

▪ GREECE IN 750 B.C.
▨ GREEK-CONTROLLED COASTS
▫ PHOENICIAN-CONTROLLED COASTS
⊗ NON-GREEK CITIES

THE OUTWARD THRUST OF A CIVILIZATION

THE GREAT AGE *of Greek expansion lasted from 750 to 550 B.C. Colonies were established along the coasts from Spain to the Black Sea. Further Greek advances to the west were halted by the well-established colonies of the older Phoenician domain, shown in blue. Expansion to the north was blocked by the fortified towns and cities of the Etruscan people of Italy. The Greek cities boxed on the map founded most of the colonies; symbols on the map identify the parent city of each of the new colonies.*

N
DNIEPER R.
SCYTHIA
DON R.
Tanais
Olbia
Tyras
Panticapaeum
Phanagoria
CRIMEA
Chersonesus
Heracleotica
COLCHIS
Istrus
Tomi
Phasis
BLACK SEA
DANUBE R.
Sinope (Sinop)
Mesembria
Amisus
Trapezus
(Trebizond)
ETRURIA
Apollonia
PAPHLAGONIA
ITALY
THRACE
PONTUS
Rome
ILLYRIA
MACEDONIA
Heraclea Pontica
BOSPORUS
Neapolis
Byzantium
Chalcedon
Cumae
(Naples)
Epidamnus
Abdera
Perinthus
BITHYNIA
Tarentum
SEA OF MARMARA
(Taranto)
Apollonia
Apollonia
Dascylium
Posidonia
Methone
Cyzicus
MAGNA
Aulon
HELLESPONT
ASIA MINOR
Elea
GRAECIA
Potidaea
Abydos
PHRYGIA
Sybaris
Callipolis
EPIRUS
Mende
Torone
MYSIA
Corcyra
AEGEAN
Hipponium
Croton
(Corfu)
Ambracia
SEA
LYDIA
Scylletium
EUBOEA
Phocaea
Himera
Messana
Leucas
IONIA
CILICIA
Mallus
(Messina)
Motya
Rhegium
ACHAEA
Megara
Soli
Selinus
(Reggio di Calabria)
CARIA
PAMPHYLIA
Corinth
GREECE
Miletus
Side
Agrigentum
Megara Hyblaea
LYCIA
PELOPONNESUS
SICILY
Syracuse
Phaselis
Citium
MELITA
CRETE
CYPRUS
SYRIA
Byblos
PHOENICIA
Sidon
MEDITERRANEAN SEA
Tyre
Cyrene
Leptis Magna
Tauchira
Barca
Saïs
Euhesperides
CYRENAICA
Naucratis
Daphnae
ARABIA
Memphis
LIBYA
EGYPT
SCALE
0
100
200
300 Miles
NILE R.
RED SEA

THE COINS OF GREECE *came from many far-flung colonies. The one above, showing the ends of a ship, is from Phaselis, famous for its seafarers.*

A SILVER PIECE *from Abdera on the fringe of the Greek world shows a seated griffin. Beyond Abdera, the legends said, was the griffins' land.*

A SYRACUSE ISSUE *celebrates triumph over Athens. A winged Victory drives a chariot. On the reverse, Persephone symbolizes abundant crops.*

APOLLO'S HEAD *adorns a coin from Abydos near Troy. The eagle, common in the mountains, was the symbol of Abydos and other nearby cities.*

A COIN OF CYRENE *displays a silphium plant. On the reverse is Zeus-Ammon—Zeus's head with the ram's horns of the Egyptian god Ammon.*

came in contact with the nomad Scyths and, although they had little in common with them, they were able to create for the Scythian market delightful gold vessels that blended Scythian subjects with Greek techniques in raised relief.

Gradually, the Greeks took full advantage of the natural resources of their adopted homes, which equaled or surpassed the native homeland in wealth. This was especially true in Sicily, where colonies like Syracuse, Selinus and Megara Hyblaea, far from being provincial, had an astonishingly vital sculpture by the mid-Sixth Century B.C. and one poet, Stesichorus, who ranked among the best of the age.

The colonies remained extensions of the homeland, for the Greeks kept apart from the culture of the indigenous peoples. Nonetheless, they made a lasting impression on many places that we do not commonly associate with Greece. Cultural integrity was not always the chief reason for remaining aloof. Colonization is frequently a dangerous business, and this was so for many Greek colonies. For a detailed account of the Greek experience we are lucky to have the personal witness of a man who participated in the colonization of the island of Thasos and the mainland of Thrace in the first part of the Seventh Century B.C. His name was Archilochus, he came from the island of Paros, and he was a gifted poet who wrote frankly and freely about his life. In fact Archilochus' frankness verged on satire, and his freedom on disillusion. He feared and disliked the "Thracian dogs" against whom he fought, but he did not have much liking or respect for his own leaders and companions. He regarded them as little better than murderers. Perhaps some of his attitudes came from his background. As the illegitimate son of a well-born adventurer and a slave, he had no rights to paternal succession and had to make his own way by his skill with the sword.

THE SCALE OF VALUES *of Athenian coins, all displaying the head of Athena, is shown here. From left to right are: a half obol, an obol, a drachma worth six obols, a double drachma and a four-drachma piece.*

Bitter, disappointed, and understandably governed by a stern sense of reality, Archilochus refused to be taken in by pretentious talk and was resolute in his desire to tell the truth, even when it hurt. His own philosophy was simple and sane: Do not rejoice too much when things go well, and when they go badly, do not lament. Paradoxically, while he rejected exaggerated expressions of the old Homeric values he also personified them in their purest sense. He believed in living honorably, regarded any material benefit as his due, earned through personal worth, and took any slight as a deadly insult. Of one who had wronged him he wrote:

> *May he be cast ashore, naked and stiff*
> *with cold, at Salmydessus and seized*
> *by Thracians (who will make him suf-*
> *fer, eating the bread of slavery), may*
> *he be covered with shellfish in the surf,*
> *may his teeth chatter like a dog's, as he*
> *lies face downwards by the margin of*
> *the waves.*

And yet he had few illusions about the efforts demanded by life and the paucity of its rewards:

> *No man gets honor or glory of his*
> *countrymen once he be dead; rather*
> *do we pursue the favor of the living*
> *while we live; the dead get ever the*
> *worst part.*

Not all Greek colonists may have been as perceptive as Archilochus, but they shared his courage and determination in setting about their task of establishing themselves in a new land. And while they bent their efforts toward this pioneering work, they also found time for artistic creativity.

Contrary to common assumption the Greeks did not have an unerring and miraculous instinct for making beautiful things. In fact they worked hard, through trial and error, before they achieved their first true successes. These came during the Seventh Century B.C., under the patronage of the aristocrats. Since the conditions of life were simple, the art that reflected them was also simple, but this did not prevent it from being noble and distinguished. Standards of proportion and balance begin to assert themselves, and the work is infused with the magical Greek light. A sense of form appears, unconsciously molded by a rocky landscape that imposes its discipline on the mind and eye.

Painting and sculpture show at once a powerful convention and many individual attempts to modify it. The Greek artist worked for a society that had strong opinions about the arts, and to some extent he had to cater to them. But within these limitations he also experimented and innovated. Looked at in the proper frame of reference, archaic Greek art is lively and varied. It ranges from life-size statues, intended to honor the gods, or the men and women who sought the gods' favor, to humble painted pots for domestic use. The first reflect Greek life at its most serious, the second at its most relaxed and gay. But gaiety and seriousness often overlapped. Statues were not required to be wholly solemn, nor was it out of order for a common drinking bowl to be decorated with dramatic or heroic subjects. Bowl and statue could each combine exaltation and delight.

As far back as Mycenaean times vases had been decorated with paintings, and the art had survived, at a much lower level, through the Dark Age. But in the Seventh Century B.C. the painting broke away from geometrical abstractions and stylized scenes. Compositions became freer and more naturalistic. Before, human figures and battles and funeral processions had been painted in formalized sets of straight lines, and the figure was no more impor-

FUNCTIONAL DESIGN *was a mark of Greek pottery. Once forms were proved suitable they were seldom varied. A few basic shapes perfected in Athens are shown above. The krater (1) had a wide mouth to facilitate mixing wine and water, the staple Greek beverage. The kylix (2) was a two-handled drinking cup. The hydria (3), for carrying water, had two horizontal handles for lifting; a third handle, not visible here, made pouring easy. The pitcher-shaped oinochoe (4) was the standard wine jug. The amphora (5) was a large urn for storing supplies. Such vases established the Mediterranean supremacy of Athenian potters.*

tant than its surroundings. Now, men and animals and monsters became the main subjects of carefully thought-out designs. New techniques were invented, new color schemes and new ways of applying paint to the clay form devised.

Drawing, at first hesitant and inexperienced, matured with astonishing speed into the flawless, expressive line which became the significant element in all Greek painting. Artists on the island of Rhodes produced animated processions of animals circling the body of a vase, and on Melos, tumultuous scenes from myths. At Sparta, during the height of that city's artistic life, soon after 600 B.C., vase paintings were delightfully diverse. There are fish in graceful patterns, dramatic episodes from the past, scenes from everyday life: Apollo kills the great serpent, Python; a dead warrior is carried home by his comrades; a king (identified as Arcesilas of Cyrene) watches the weighing and packing of silphium, a medicinal plant much prized in the ancient world. Continuously experimenting, artists learned how to use empty space to stress the contours of a figure, how to compose groups of men and women into a continuous procession, how to mass them without crowding. Even the vase itself became an element of the design, as the artist adapted his subject to fit its particular curves and protuberances.

In sculpture, development came later and had further to go. Small figurines in clay or bronze provided a beginning in the Dark Age. And then, in the Seventh Century B.C., larger figures appeared, in wood, limestone, marble and bronze. The earliest Greek monumental sculpture obviously owed a great deal to Egyptian example. The Greeks began with upright figures of naked men and clothed women, life-size and carved in the round. The men have one foot forward and their arms hang down at their sides. The women are heavily draped in what looks, in the earliest examples, like mere layers of cloth. But the Egyptian stiffness is left behind with remarkable speed. The male form becomes more engaging, mainly through the balance of its limbs and the treatment of its muscles. And the female form gains in grace as its draperies become lighter and more delicate, hinting at the body beneath.

But sculpture was not confined to figures in the round. Carved decorations also began to appear on the architectural elements of temples: in the triangular space under the roof, called the pediment; on the band between the roof and columns, known as the frieze, which in certain instances included rectangles called metopes, spaced at intervals. Each of these shapes—triangle, band, rectangle—raised special design problems. The pediment, for example, would take a full human figure in the center, but something else was required for the acute angles at its base. The frieze had to be a continuous pattern but could not be too crowded or busy with detail. And the metopes had to have a composition that neatly filled the rigid confines of a rectangle.

Not all of these problems were solved at once, but the principal ones were under control by the end of the Sixth Century B.C. By this time the Greek artist had learned to discipline his feeling for form to suit the requirements of a severe frame. He knew how to balance his component parts. His work became richer in detail and more dramatic. And the sculptural details reveal, as the economical line in the vase paintings cannot, how much the Greeks knew about the human figure.

As the visual arts progressed from rude beginnings to majestic maturity, poetry also evolved new forms. The impersonal epic, with its heroic sentiments, gave way to a poetry whose sentiments were often quite personal and whose subject matter was often current events. This was the golden age of lyric song, of poems sung to the accompaniment of the flute or the lyre. Sometimes the performers were individuals, sometimes choruses. The music

itself is known only through isolated fragments, but the surviving words enchant the ear with their effortless, dancing rhythms.

Lyric poetry had many uses and took many forms. It could, for instance, be a powerful instrument in public affairs. The Spartan poet Tyrtaeus, active in the mid-Seventh Century B.C., wrote stirring military songs, exhorting his countrymen to battle and indoctrinating them with the glories of war. In Athens another poet, Solon, who lived from about 640 to 560 B.C., preached a philosophy of social reform to a city torn by dissension—and actually got some of his reforms enacted when he became a leader of the state.

Sometimes lyric poetry was composed in the form of choral works—combining music, poetry and dance—for performance at civic festivals. At one time Sparta was a center of such festivals, and one of its most famous poets was a man named Alcman who, late in the Seventh Century B.C., wrote lyrics for choruses of young Spartan women. His poems are wonderfully limpid and gay, entirely suited to his performers:

> Look, beside me sings my friend,
> my cousin, of the ankles small:
> Agido and she commend
> alike our ceremonial.
> Immortals, who possess the end
> of every action, hear their call
> with favor, as their voices blend!

Some of the best of the lyric poems were written by poets about themselves for their friends. The highest point of this personal lyric poetry was reached about 600 B.C. on the island of Lesbos in the work of two poets, a man and a woman. The thoroughly masculine Alcaeus wrote about politics and war and the pleasures of wine-drinking. His friend Sappho wrote about her feelings for the

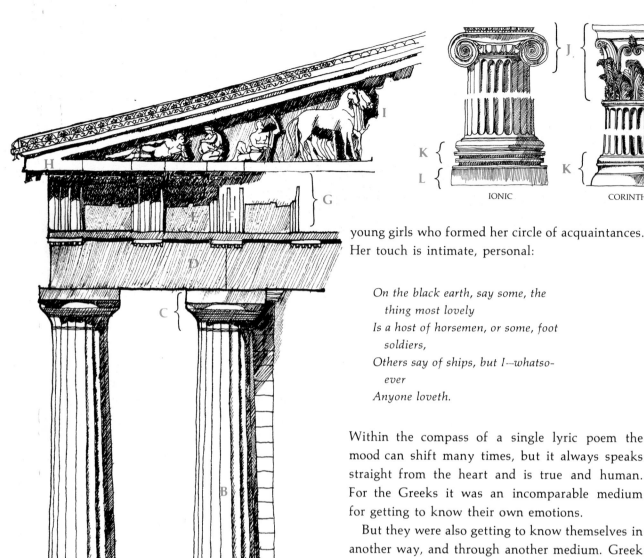

DORIC

IONIC   CORINTHIAN

THREE ARCHITECTURAL STYLES *of Greece's temples and their principal parts are illustrated above. The letters indicate: (A) the steps and stylobate, or platform, of the temple; (B) the fluted column shaft; (C) the cushion (echinus) and rectangular block (abacus) which together form the capital; (D) the architrave, which performs the function of a beam; (E) the plain or sculptured metope tablets; (F) the projecting and channeled triglyph tablets; (G) the frieze, comprising the metope and triglyph tablets; (H) the projecting cornice; and (I) the pediment, or sculptured gable, between the sloping roof surfaces. At (J) are shown the voluted capital of an Ionic column (left) and the acanthus-leafed capital of the Corinthian style (right); (K) the molded bases of the two styles; and (L) the plinth, or supporting block of stone, used in some Ionic-style temples. Some temples combined features of different styles.*

young girls who formed her circle of acquaintances. Her touch is intimate, personal:

> On the black earth, say some, the
>   thing most lovely
> Is a host of horsemen, or some, foot
>   soldiers,
> Others say of ships, but I—whatso-
>   ever
> Anyone loveth.

Within the compass of a single lyric poem the mood can shift many times, but it always speaks straight from the heart and is true and human. For the Greeks it was an incomparable medium for getting to know their own emotions.

But they were also getting to know themselves in another way, and through another medium. Greek religion, as it is revealed in poetry, always encouraged inquiry into the nature of things. Curiosity was pleasing to the gods because curiosity made the gods' marvelous works known to men. The myths had in their time done much to explain the world to unsophisticated people, but now something more factual and more precise was needed. And so science and philosophy were born. As early as the Sixth Century B.C., Ionian Greeks were seeking a primal substance, a single basic material from which, they reasoned, all other things must have developed. Three men, all of them from Miletus, and all of them astronomers and mathematicians, had theories about it. Thales thought that the basic material was a clear liquid; Anaximenes thought that it was a colorless gas; and Anaximander thought it was some indeterminate substance, boundless and imperishable. At the same time another group of men, also Ionians, were speculating on the nature of life itself. They were seeking a single, unifying principle that would explain why things are what they are.

One of these men was Heraclitus, who lived in Ephesus. Heraclitus believed that the essential condition of life was "flux"—that nothing was absolute, everything changed. Pythagoras, who was born on Samos but lived most of his life in the Greek colony of Croton in Italy, believed that the universe was ordered by a harmonious system of numbers. One of his concepts has come down to us as the Pythagorean theorem, which proves that the sum of the squares of the two shorter sides of a right-angled triangle is equal to the square of the long side. The third of these early philosophers was Xenophanes, who was driven from his home in Ionia by a Persian invasion and settled at Elea in Italy. Xenophanes founded a philosophical school which taught that the universe was ordered by a single, supreme, divine being who operated through thought alone.

Although these early scientists and philosophers attached the utmost importance to their work, and did not hesitate to reject the old myths about the gods if the myths were at variance with their theories, they still believed in some divine governance of the world. If they had to discredit an old myth, they created a new one to take its place. Their methods were not what we should call scientific. Working at the very dawn of science, they operated largely by flashes of insight and inspired guesses. Nevertheless some of their conclusions are astonishing. Anaximander, for instance, claimed that the world was but one in an unending succession of worlds; and Xenophanes declared that man had originally come out of the sea, and produced fossils as evidence.

To the aristocratic elite, the pursuit of scientific knowledge gave as much pleasure as the enjoyment of fine arts. They made no distinction between the love of beauty and the love of truth. And yet this apparently enlightened society was troubled by persistent conflict. Life was pleasant for the aristocrats, but for the peasants and slaves it was often hard indeed.

Many of the poor were regularly on the very edge of starvation, and naturally turned on the rich, demanding land and power. They enjoyed occasional successes but these seldom produced any lasting victory. Consequently Greece was continually disturbed by civil strife. Sometimes the two factions were so at odds that the government became powerless, leaving the way clear for some able or unscrupulous man to force his way to the top and take over. Such men, known as tyrants, produced at least some sort of equilibrium. The best of them even tried to conciliate the warring factions. Tyrants frequently made concessions to the poorer classes, and in return counted on their support to keep themselves in power.

In reality, tyrannies were extensions of the aristocratic system. Under them the city-state gained even greater unity than before, enabling it to resist attack. And because power was concentrated in one man's hands, public works and enterprises could be undertaken on a scale that would otherwise have been impossible. Some tyrants, it is true, were brutal and unjust and gave "tyrant" the unpleasant connotation it has today. But others were beneficent and law-abiding. The tyrants epitomized the spirit of a vigorous but divided society. They reflected its tastes and temperament, and their unusual power gave them unusual opportunities to display its salient traits in action.

During the Seventh and Sixth Centuries B.C. most city-states conformed to this changing pattern of aristocratic life. But one city eventually moved beyond the pattern, and one never turned its back on the aristocratic ways. And again, the two cities were Athens and Sparta.

Although Sparta had a cultural flowering, it did not last very long and it did not alter the old Spartan institutions. Remnants of the city's period of grace and elegance continued into the Sixth Century; they can be seen in painted pots and carved ivories. But Sparta stood obdurately outside the main currents of economic change. In the Seventh Century, when Lydia introduced coinage to the entire Greek world, thereby simplifying the whole economic structure, Sparta refused to conform and continued to use cumbersome iron rods as monetary exchange. Sparta refused to take up commerce on any serious scale, preferring to remain an agrarian society, dependent on serf labor. It continued to practice the arts of war, even in peace. Its fidelity to its old ways was based partly on fear: Spartan citizens were heavily outnumbered by their slaves and serfs. Consequently they insisted on maintaining their old camp discipline and, unlike any other Greek city, remained a military community.

For a greater part of this same period Athens conformed to the general pattern. From 561 to 527 B.C. it was governed by a gifted tyrant, Peisistratus. Though himself an aristocrat, he rose to power by promising to liberalize the land laws, and did so. He was exiled twice when opposition factions briefly regained power, but in both instances he managed to return. Peisistratus beautified the city, supported the art of poetry, encouraged drama and, in the latter years of his rule, commissioned a learned body to prepare a definitive text of the *Iliad* and the *Odyssey*. Under his leadership Athens strengthened its ties with Ionia, giving the city greater influence in the Aegean area.

When he died, Peisistratus was succeeded by his sons, Hippias and Hipparchus, but they lacked their father's tact and talents. In 514 B.C., Hippar-chus, the younger son, was murdered, and in 510 B.C., Hippias was expelled by a group of Athenian nobles who had gone into exile during his father's time in office. The exiles were helped by Sparta, which undoubtedly thought that the tyranny would be succeeded by a government more to its taste. But in fact the overthrow of Hippias led to a revolutionary change that was not welcome to Sparta.

In 507 B.C. the Athenian constitution was remodeled by a brilliant reformer, Cleisthenes, who was a member of a noble family active in Athenian politics. Under the new constitution all adult male citizens were automatically members of the Assembly and had a say in public affairs. Athenians claimed with justice that their government offered equality before the laws, equality of power and freedom of speech. If it was not the full democracy it later became, it contained the mechanics for ultimately becoming one. With their newly acquired political freedom the Athenians felt a miraculous surge of confidence and strength.

Troubled by these developments, the Spartans in 506 B.C. invaded Attica, but the Athenians drove them off. Then, inflamed by their new belief in themselves, the Athenians went on to annex the territory of Oropus on their northern coast and acquire the rich plain of Chalcis across the strait at Aulis. They also attacked the island of Aegina, which lies in full view of Athens in the Saronic Gulf, but they failed to subdue it.

Nevertheless, the Athenians were obviously on the move. Once but a single state among many, with no special pre-eminence, Athens now began the career which was to make it the most energetic and influential power in the Greek world. The full results were not to appear immediately because, for a dramatic and crowded interval, one urgent problem occupied the attention alike of Athens, Sparta and most other Greek cities: they had to survive the Persian Wars.

THE LIGHT OF GREECE, *which seems to be brighter and more lustrous than light elsewhere, slants down on the Argive plain. The wall is part of ancient Mycenae, where the war against Troy was planned.*

THE GREEK HOMELAND

The hard, clear Greek light, playing on glittering water, bright white limestone and bare brown earth, impresses every new beholder. This clarity, admirers of the Greeks suggest, may have determined the hard, direct quality of Greek thought. And it infuses an essentially harsh landscape with glowing beauty. The Greek mainland is a stiff 300-mile-long finger pointing southeast into the seas. On this peninsula the lives of the people were shaped by their dwelling places: on rugged mountain slopes, in the dry valleys, along the gulfs and on islands. The climate tested them: the mountain winters were bitter, the lowland summers hot and dusty. But winter or summer, the Greek found joy in spending as much time as possible out of doors.

A BOUNCY HUNTER *strides homeward with his kill slung behind him and his dog dancing ahead on a lead. His weapons were spears, nets, foot-snares, javelins and, infrequently, the bow and arrow.*

A TUMBLING COUNTRYSIDE, *Greece's mountains (above) helped the city-states to develop independently of one another. These heights, the Arakhnaions in the Peloponnesus, separated Epidaurus from Argos.*

THE ROUGH HIGHLANDS

Although walled in separate communities by mountains, plains and seas, the Greeks were never far from one another; no man in Greece stood more than 60 miles from the sea. Of the three areas, the mountains and barren regions, covering three quarters of the country, offered poorest fare. Once these ridges were covered with scrub forests but by the Fifth Century B.C., the slopes had few trees left. The country's bones showed. Lack of moisture in the mountains and the fondness of goats for saplings had produced a sparse Greece. The highlands offered aromatic plants for honeybees (important in a sugarless land); hunting for hare, lynx, bear, wolves and lions (if only to protect the flocks); and summer grazing for sheep and goats, which were the source of Greek cloaks and Greek cheeses.

A FOUNTAIN OF ROCKS, *the grotesque pillars of Meteora (below), sculptured by ages of wind and water, range from 85 to 300 feet high. Ancient Greeks believed that they were rocks flung down on the earth by angry gods.*

A ROADSIDE COPSE *in the mountains lying between Sparta and Kalamata is filled with cypresses and small growth. In this area, a famous hunting ground, Spartans abandoned children deemed too weak to become soldiers.*

VENERABLE GROVES *of gnarled-trunk olive trees (left) offer a spectacular show when their leaves flash from silvery grey to white as the dry summer wind rustles the branches.*

ON THESSALY'S PLAINS *sheep graze in peace (below). These animals, whose wool provided essential warm clothing, were often covered with skins to keep their fleece soft.*

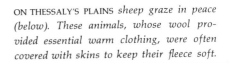

TASSELED WHEAT *ripens in the Greek sunlight. Although they raised some grain each year, the Athenians failed to raise enough in most years. They had to buy in Egypt and the Crimea to fill their storage bins.*

THE FRUITFUL VALLEYS

Between the mountains were fertile pockets. Although they made up less than a quarter of all the land, their soil was deep and level. Here grew the "Mediterranean triad": grain; grapes for wine, the Greek drink much in demand overseas; and olives, whose oil was the butter, soap and lamp fuel of antiquity. Large-scale olive growing was left to gentlemen. Only they had the capital to wait the 16 years until a tree matured and only they had the patience for the 40 years needed to bring it to peak production. After that a man could sit back and enjoy himself.

A SACRIFICIAL CALF *is carried to a shrine. The Greeks' meager supply of meat came in the main from such votive offerings.*

A BROAD THOROUGHFARE TO THE WORLD

Living on a peninsula, the Greeks came early to the sea. They panned it for salt, then set sail upon it in boats to catch tunny, mullet, anchovies and sardines, develop trade routes to the Greek islands and the mainland of Asia Minor, drive the Phoenicians away and defeat the Persians. They found courses through the windy raceways of the Dardanelles and Bosporus to the Black Sea, routes that do not differ much from modern sailing directions. They remained cautious seamen; they sailed by day, anchored by night and stayed ashore in the winter. They talked nervously of being caught between the rock of Scylla and the whirlpool of Charybdis off Italy's boot. Legend has it that an adventurous Greek sailor from Marseilles discovered the Tin Islands (presumably England, whose mines in Cornwall were a principal source of tin until the last century). But the prudent Greeks, awed by Carthaginian strength in the western Mediterranean and the Atlantic, never challenged the North Africans' long supremacy in the tin trade.

HOME WATERS OF THE GREEKS, *the Aegean Sea is dotted with islands and headlands. Navigators moved from one to the next, always trying to keep some familiar piece of land in sight.*

LORD OF WIND AND WAVES, *Poseidon, god of the sea, lifts a balancing hand as he prepares to throw a trident. The Greeks believed that on the water their fate rested with Poseidon.*

ΠΕΛΛΑΣ

ΔΑΡΕΙΟΣ

ΠΕΡΣΑΙ

ΜΥΗΡΟΣΙ

4
THE PERSIAN WARS

IN A COUNCIL OF WAR *Persia's King Darius, on the throne, decides to invade Greece. This work was made by a Greek artist in southern Italy about 325 B.C. Above Darius are gods; below, Persians bringing tribute.*

While the young Greek culture gathered strength and assurance, another culture, to the east, was also expanding its power. Unlike the Greeks, with their insistence on individual freedom, the Persians submitted to a ruler whose power was absolute. The Greeks were soon to be challenged by the Persian autocracy, and to learn that freedom, to be preserved, must sometimes be curtailed. It was a lesson they learned slowly, and on occasion the fate of Western civilization hung upon the outcome of petty disputes among Greek city-states.

For many centuries the Greek colonial cities on the coast of Asia Minor had very little trouble with the great states to the east. The power of Babylonia and Assyria never reached that far west. In the first half of the Seventh Century B.C., however, a Lydian king, Gyges, attacked the Greek cities in the course of expanding his inland kingdom to the coast. Later Lydian kings allowed them autonomy, but not complete freedom from Lydian rule. The last of the Lydian kings, Croesus, who made himself the richest monarch of his time by exploiting his country's gold deposits, admired the Greeks greatly. He sent royal gifts to the famous shrine of Apollo at Delphi, home of a revered oracle and the most venerable sanctuary in Greece.

In 546 B.C., Croesus was attacked and defeated by Cyrus the Great, King of Persia. Cyrus had already combined Persia, Media and Assyria into one vast dominion. Croesus tried to stop him, and expected to succeed, because the Delphic oracle had told him that he would "destroy a great empire." He assumed that the empire meant was Cyrus', but instead, he destroyed his own. Afterwards Croesus is said to have commented sadly, "No one is so foolish as to prefer to peace war, in which, instead of sons burying their fathers, fathers bury their sons. But the gods willed it so."

After conquering the Lydians, Cyrus marched his well-trained army to the coast and subdued all of the major Ionian colonies except the island of Samos, which held out under the determined leadership of its tyrant, Polycrates. Polycrates combined piratical control of the sea with lavish patronage of the arts. He plundered friend and foe alike, but then returned his friends' property—on the theory that they would be more grateful than if they had been spared in the first place. He was also a pioneer in engineering works, commissioning a breakwater to be built for his harbor and a tunnel to be dug through a mountain for his water supply. But he was no match for the Persians, who lured him to the Asian mainland in 520 B.C. and crucified him. Darius I, who had succeeded to the Persian throne the year before, was now master of all Ionia.

The Persians did not allow their new subjects to retain their autonomy. They made local tyrants subordinate to Persian provincial governors, called satraps, and forced the Ionians to pay tribute and do military service. The Greeks of the mainland, across the Aegean, did very little to halt the subjugation. Sparta did make a gesture: it sent envoys to the Persians, protesting their actions and reminding them that Sparta claimed the right to protect all Greek cities. But it failed to follow up the protest with effective action. The other cities on the Greek mainland did not even protest.

For a time the Ionians submitted to the Persian regime, even though they did not take kindly to it. But in 499 B.C., they revolted. This time Athens sent 20 shiploads of soldiers to help, and Eretria, on the island of Euboea, sent five. The Ionians began promisingly enough by advancing inland to the city of Sardis and burning it. After this initial sally, however, the Athenian and Eretrian allies went home, and the Ionians were left to their own resources. For a while they stubbornly struggled on alone, but ultimately the revolt collapsed. The final engagement was a naval battle off the island of Lade, near Miletus, in which, according to the historian Herodotus, a fleet of 353 Ionian ships was overwhelmed by a fleet of 600 ships in the service of Persia—but Herodotus may have exaggerated the latter figure.

To chastise the Greeks for this uprising the Persians sacked and burned Miletus, and transplanted part of its population to the mouth of the Tigris

A SOLDIER'S GEAR *included many things useful or merely cumbersome. The bronze helmet (above), usually adorned with a crest of dyed horsehair, restricted both side vision and hearing but protected the head. The bronze tip of the battering ram with the ram's head cast on it (below) was meant for use against city walls, though it seldom succeeded. The short sword and the lance whose metal point is shown at right were the principal weapons.*

River on the Persian Gulf, more than a thousand miles away. It was a terrible blow to the Greeks. Miletus had been the richest and most brilliant of the Ionian cities, with more than 60 colonies of its own, ranging from the Adriatic to the Hellespont. Shortly after its destruction, when the Athenian poet Phrynichus turned its story into a tragedy, *The Capture of Miletus*, his Athenian audience wept so bitterly that the playwright was fined 1,000 drachmas for depressing them.

From his capital at Susa, Darius had followed the course of the whole Ionian revolt, and probably did not fail to note the desertion of the Greek mainland troops after Sardis. On the basis of this show of weakness, as well as his own strength, the subjection of the Greeks must have seemed a small affair to him. Darius was the sole ruler of a vast empire which extended from Egypt to India, and from the Persian Gulf to the Black Sea, an area of more than two million square miles. The ruins of the royal palace at Persepolis display his image in relief over the doorways, proclaiming his omnipotence under the protection of Ahura Mazda, the chief Persian god. Sculptured processions of soldiers, officials, tributaries and slaves march in friezes along the palace stairways, acknowledging their subservience to him as the Great King.

Darius was more than an Oriental despot, however. He was a shrewd and aggressive leader, astute in money matters and interested in engineering. His contemporaries called him "The Huckster," for, says Herodotus, "Darius looked to making a gain in everything." He gave his name to the daric, the gold coin that was the basis of his currency, and he supported his national economy by fixed yearly taxes. He built a canal between the Nile and the Red Sea, and built a network of roads for the movement of his armies. One of these highways, the Royal Road, ran 1,500 miles from Susa, near the Persian Gulf, to Sardis, near the Aegean. One of the most important

functionaries in Darius' court was the man who supervised these roads, an official called the "King's Eye."

In 492 B.C., Darius made his first move against the Greek mainland. He sent a large force of men and ships under the leadership of his son-in-law Mardonius to subdue Thrace and Macedonia, and then, if possible, to move southward into the Greek peninsula. Mardonius accomplished the first part of his task, but wrecked his ships rounding Mt. Athos in Macedonia and had to return home.

Darius now sent heralds to all the Greek states, demanding their submission and token gifts of "earth and water." Some states complied, but not Athens and Sparta. According to Herodotus the Athenians threw the Persian heralds in a pit, suggesting that they collect their own earth, and Sparta threw them into a well, suggesting they collect their own water. But although the two states rejected the Persian demands, they did nothing to forestall Persian action. Athens was busy working out the problems of a democratic form of government—and casting covetous eyes on its neighbors. Sparta, with its two kings, was almost literally of two minds about the Persian menace.

In 490 B.C., Darius struck again. He sent two generals, Datis and Artaphernes, across the Aegean with a fleet of 600 ships and a large and well-equipped army; they sailed for the bay of Marathon, intending to land their troops and to march overland to Athens. But they held their ships offshore, in case it became necessary to sail around and attack Athens through its port of Phaleron.

With the enemy on their own soil the Athenians suddenly awoke to their danger. In a remarkably successful instance of hurried, last-minute planning, they decided on a strategy and tactics that turned out to be flawless. Most of the credit for these plans must go to an able and determined general named Miltiades, who had been the governor

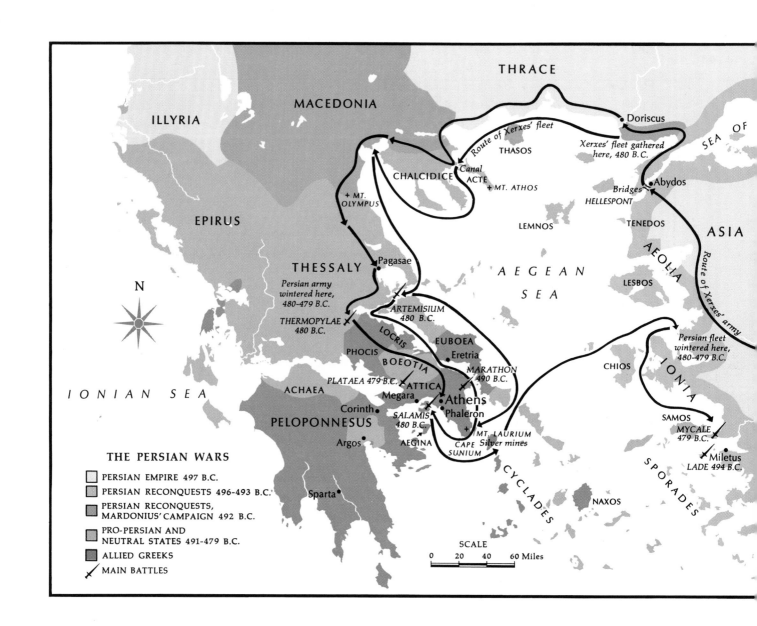

THRACE

ILLYRIA

MACEDONIA

Route of Xerxes' fleet

• Doriscus

THASOS

Xerxes' fleet gathered here, 480 B.C.

SEA OF

Canal
ACTE
CHALCIDICE

+ MT. ATHOS

Bridges•
HELLESPONT
•Abydos

+ MT.
OLYMPUS

EPIRUS

LEMNOS

TENEDOS

ASIA

AEOLIA

Route of Xerxes' army

THESSALY
•Pagasae

Persian army wintered here, 480-479 B.C.

A E G E A N

S E A

N

LESBOS

ARTEMISIUM 480 B.C.

THERMOPYLAE
480 B.C.

LOCRIS

PHOCIS

EUBOEA
•Eretria

BOEOTIA

MARATHON 490 B.C.

Persian fleet wintered here, 480-479 B.C.

CHIOS

I O N I A N   S E A

ACHAEA

PLATAEA 479 B.C. ATTICA
Megara•

Corinth•

PELOPONNESUS

•Argos

SALAMIS 480 B.C.

AEGINA

•Athens
•Phaleron

+ MT. LAURIUM
Silver mines

CAPE
SUNIUM

IONIA

SAMOS

MYCALE 479 B.C.

•Miletus
LADE 494 B.C.

SPORADES

•Sparta

C Y C L A D E S

NAXOS

THE PERSIAN WARS

☐ PERSIAN EMPIRE 497 B.C.
◼ PERSIAN RECONQUESTS 496-493 B.C.
◼ PERSIAN RECONQUESTS,
   MARDONIUS' CAMPAIGN 492 B.C.
◼ PRO-PERSIAN AND
   NEUTRAL STATES 491-479 B.C.
◼ ALLIED GREEKS
✕ MAIN BATTLES

SCALE
0   20   40   60 Miles

THE EBB AND FLOW OF BATTLE

THE GREAT CONFLICT *between Greeks and Persians, whose main battles and campaigns are outlined on the map above, involved most of the peoples of the Near East. When Xerxes led his formations across the Hellespont, Herodotus says, they included not only his Medes and Persians armored in iron scales but also other troops variously attired: Assyrians who wore brass helmets and Moschians who wore wooden ones; straight-haired eastern Ethiopians with helmets made of horses' scalps, and curly-haired western Ethiopians who dressed in leopard and lion skins and painted their bodies half chalk, half vermilion. The Indians in the line of march wore cotton dresses and carried bows of cane, while the Scyths were clad in trousers and tall, pointed caps and fought with bows, daggers and battle axes. The Thracians dressed in long cloaks of many colors. But the most spectacular unit in the army was the Ten Thousand, a body of picked Persians sometimes called the Immortals because when one fell in battle he was immediately replaced by another. They marched glittering with gold decorations and were followed by servants and women.*

BLACK SEA

MARMARA

MINOR

◄Sardis
*Xerxes' army
wintered here,
481-480 B.C.*

of a Thracian city and, as such, had firsthand acquaintance with Persian battle tactics. He persuaded his fellow generals not to wait for the Persians to attack, but to take the offensive and march immediately to meet them at Marathon. His purpose was partly to save as much of the countryside as possible from devastation, and partly to thwart possible traitors.

At Marathon, a plain hemmed in by mountains and sea, Miltiades took the initiative and ordered his infantry to advance at a run and in close order for a distance, Herodotus says, of a "little under a mile." It was a new tactic for the Greeks, and apparently astounded the Persians, who, according to Herodotus, "when they saw the Greeks coming on at speed," without the support of horsemen or archers, "made ready to receive them, although it seemed to them that the Athenians were bereft of their senses, and bent upon their own destruction." But the onslaught was more than the Persians could deal with. They fell back to their ships or into the sea. Herodotus claims that Marathon cost the Persians 6,400 men to the Athenians' 192.

Miltiades dispatched a runner to Athens with the news of the victory, and hurried his army back to meet the Persian forces now advancing on Phaleron by ship. When the Persians rounded Cape Sunium and neared the shore they found him holding such a commanding position that it was impossible for them to land, and so they withdrew and sailed home. The runner meanwhile had run nonstop the whole distance from Marathon to Athens, 22 miles, to gasp out his message, "We have been victorious!" and fall dead. To Athenians the victory was so astonishing that they could only explain it by assuming that gods and heroes had fought on their side. The dead of Marathon were buried in a great commemorative mound, which still stands at the site of the battle, and its veterans were held in high honor all their lives.

For the next 10 years the Greeks had a respite; Persia was occupied with other matters—changes resulting from the death of Darius, and a revolt in Egypt. But Darius' son Xerxes, who succeeded to the throne in 485 B.C., was determined to pursue his father's plan. For years a slave stood beside him at dinner and whispered, "Master, remember the Athenians." Xerxes' preparations were even more thorough than his father's. In a prodigious feat for the time, he had a canal dug through the neck of the Mt. Athos peninsula, where the ships of his father's first expedition had been wrecked.

Athens, meanwhile, was embroiled in internal squabbles among political leaders, and in military forays against the neighboring island of Aegina, then the strongest naval power in Greece. Gradually, as more people acquired voting rights and the power of the popular Assembly increased, the power of the aristocracy faded. Finally one man of the people became the leading voice in the Athenian democracy. Themistocles was the personification of the vigorous Athenian spirit. Vehement and impetuous as a youth, quick to learn, and with a strong bent for action and public affairs, he was the very model of a politician and apparently knew it. As a young man he said, "I shall enter politics and persuade my way to the top." And later: "I cannot tune a harp, but I know how to take a modest city in hand and raise it to greatness."

Themistocles thought that the future of Athens lay in sea power, a notion that naturally got strong support from those elements of the population that lived by seafaring. As far back as 493 B.C. he had conceived the idea of building a new harbor for Athens at Piraeus, which was much easier to fortify than the existing harbor at Phaleron. In fact he had already started to build a protective wall around Piraeus before the Persian attack. After the Persian retreat he persuaded the Assembly to finish it. Then, when a rich vein of silver was discovered in the

southern part of Attica, he also persuaded the Assembly to expand the navy. This was accomplished just before Xerxes began to move in 480 B.C.

Thanks to Themistocles' advice, Athens was far better prepared than any other Greek state for the coming crisis. Yet such was the reputation of Sparta in military matters that it was to Sparta, rather than Athens, that the Greeks turned for leadership against Xerxes. In 481 B.C., at Sparta's invitation, representatives of all the Greek states met and agreed to terminate their feuds in the interest of their common danger. Calling themselves the League of the Greeks, they gave Sparta authority over all their forces. At first the League considered massing its troops at the Isthmus of Corinth, the narrow neck of land that joins the Peloponnesus to the rest of Greece. But this plan was rejected because it would have abandoned central and northern Greece to the enemy, and thereby exposed Athens directly to the Persians.

The Greeks then decided to make a stand near the northern border of Thessaly, but this left them unprotected in the rear. So they withdrew instead to the narrow pass at Thermopylae, on the southern border of Thessaly—a wise military move, but foolish politically. Thinking itself abandoned, all of northern Greece submitted to the enemy, and this in turn aroused the defeatist elements within the Greek ranks. These elements felt that effective resistance to Xerxes' army, with its enormous reserves of manpower and materials, was impossible. They thought that the wisest course was to make peace on the best terms they could get, and claimed support for their views in the utterances of the Delphic oracle, a profound influence on temporal as well as spiritual affairs.

The oracle first announced that resistance was hopeless, and warned Athens and Sparta that they would be destroyed. A second response was less harsh, but ambiguous:

*Then far-seeing Zeus grants this to the
    prayers of Athena;
Safe shall the wooden wall continue for
    thee and thy children.*

Athens and Sparta chose to make this mean that defense was possible, although "wooden walls" might mean a palisade or might mean the hulls of ships. The two states still disagreed on policy, however. Sparta continued to press for a defense confined to the Peloponnesus, and Athens had to force the Spartan generals to change their minds by threatening to withdraw the Athenian fleet.

Xerxes had been proceeding toward Europe with a fighting force that Herodotus puts at a staggering total of 2,641,610 men, supported by 1,207 warships and 3,000 smaller vessels. Most modern historians think, however, that the Persian army probably numbered between 150,000 and 200,000 combat troops, and its navy probably consisted of 700 to 800 warships. When he reached the Hellespont, Xerxes ordered his engineers to build him a bridge, but it tore apart in a storm. At this, says Herodotus, Xerxes was ". . . full of wrath, and straightway gave orders that the Hellespont should receive 300 lashes, and that a pair of fetters should be cast into it . . . I have even heard it said, that he bade the branders take their irons and therewith brand the Hellespont. It is certain that he commanded those who scourged the waters to utter, as they lashed them . . . barbarian and wicked words . . . he likewise commanded that the overseers of the work should lose their heads." Other overseers were set to work on a second set of bridges, and this time they succeeded. One bridge had 314 boats lashed together, the other 360; they spanned something over a mile and a quarter. The roadway was lined on either side with bulwarks that hid the sea from view so that the horses and beasts of burden would not take fright.

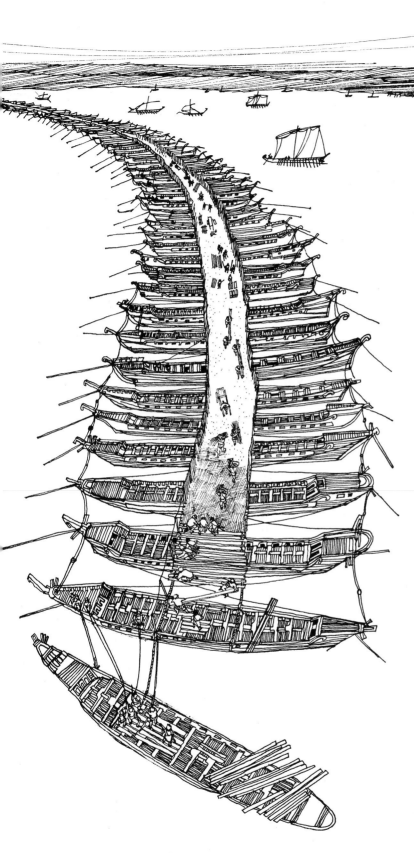

After he had crossed the Hellespont, Xerxes advanced into Greece by the classic invasion route, marching for the most part parallel to the shore, so that the Persian ships could provide support and supplies. When he reached Thermopylae, then a narrow, 50-foot-wide defile between the mountains and the sea (but now broadened by silt from a nearby river to a plain that is in some places three miles wide), Xerxes met an advance force of the Greek army. Three hundred Spartan warriors had marched north under their king, Leonidas, expecting the rest of their allies to follow at the conclusion of the Olympic Games, which took place at the same time. En route, Leonidas had picked up more than 6,000 additional men, so that by the time he reached his destination his full strength was some 7,000.

For four days Xerxes waited, while the long line of Persian cavalry and infantry marched into position at Thermopylae. During this period he sent a spy to observe the enemy camp and, Herodotus says, laughed in disdain when the spy reported that the Spartans spent their time doing gymnastic exercises and combing their long hair. But one of Xerxes' advisers corrected his impression. He explained to Xerxes that it was a custom among the Spartans "when they are about to hazard their lives, to adorn their heads with care . . ." and told him that in fact the Persians were about to face the "first kingdom and town in Greece, and with the bravest men."

On the fifth and sixth days after he had arrived at the pass, Xerxes attacked. Making no headway, he "leaped three times from his throne in agony for his army." But from this point on, the battle took a different turn and acquired the desperate, magnificent character of all heroic struggles against hopeless odds. A Greek traitor showed the Persians a way through the mountains, enabling them to strike at the Greeks from the rear. Responding swiftly, Leonidas sent the main body of the Greek army

XERXES' BRIDGES *over the Hellespont are shown in a drawing based on research by modern military experts. The boats are pentekonters, or 50-oared galleys. They were anchored fore and aft and lashed in line 9 to 11 feet apart. Roadways were made of thick planks resting on large cables suspended from the boats and covered with straw matting and dirt.*

back to safety, but with his own 300 Spartans and a picked group of allies, determined to hold the pass. He attacked and was killed almost instantly. "And now there arose," says Herodotus, "a fierce struggle between the Persians and the Lacedaemonians over the body of Leonidas, in which the Greeks four times drove back the enemy, and at last by their great bravery succeeded in bearing off the body." The Greeks fought on, leaderless, but in the end were left with nothing but a hillock. Here, says Herodotus, "they defended themselves to the last, such as still had swords using them, and the others resisting with their hands and teeth; till the barbarians . . . overwhelmed and buried the remnant left beneath showers of missile weapons."

With Thermopylae taken, Xerxes moved across central Greece unopposed, toward Athens and the second phase of the war. Instead of preparing to defend that city, however, the Greek armies returned to their original scheme—to fortify themselves at the Corinthian Isthmus. Left at the mercy of the Persians, Athens had to be evacuated. Themistocles ordered the women and children to be sent to Aegina, Salamis and Troezen for safety, and recruited all the remaining able-bodied men for the Greek navy, for which he now had new plans. He proposed to engage the enemy at sea, and so compel them to retire by land.

In the general confusion of the Athenian evacuation, Plutarch writes, "many old men, by reason of their great age, were left behind; and even the tame domestic animals could not be seen without some pity, running about the town and howling, as desirous to be carried along with their masters that had kept them; among which it is reported that Xanthippus, the father of Pericles, had a dog that would not endure to stay behind, but leaped into the sea, and swam along by the galley's side till he came to the island of Salamis, where he fainted away and died."

While Xerxes, moving according to plan, took Athens, Themistocles was engaged in political manipulations designed to bring the Greek navy into combat with the Persian fleet. Most of the Peloponnesian commanders wanted the Greek ships to be moved to the western end of the Saronic Gulf, just offshore from the Isthmus, where their army was gathered. But Themistocles was determined to keep the fleet at Salamis and fight in the narrow channel between the island and the mainland, not far from Athens. He thought that the narrowness of the channel would give him a tactical advantage, but he also had another motive in choosing it. He was anxious to stop the Persians before they penetrated too deeply into Greek waters. If the Persian fleet could be defeated at a point close to Athens, Xerxes might be forced to retire from that city as well.

Themistocles finally got the Greek commanders to agree to his plan, and then duped the Persians into attacking him. He secretly sent a trusted slave to the Persians with a message pretending sympathy and warning them that the Greek fleet was frightened and meant to run away without fighting. Xerxes responded to this as Themistocles had hoped he would: he closed in on the Greek fleet, and the battle of Salamis was begun. In some ways Salamis anticipated Sir Francis Drake's famous rout of the Spanish Armada, nearly 21 centuries later. The Persian ships greatly outnumbered the Greek, but they were actually hampered by this. They could not move easily in the narrow waters, got in each other's way and lost whatever unity of command they might have had. The Greek ships, on the other hand, though fewer in number, were better manned and managed, smaller and easier to maneuver, and in addition were fitted with rams. They darted among the Persians, harrying them and driving them against each other. Then, with the help of a favoring wind, they forced them to retreat, sailing around them, as they went, to pick off stragglers.

For the Persians it was an enormous rout. The sea was choked with the wreckage of ships and slaughtered men, and the coast was piled high with dead. From the shore, Xerxes watched the carnage, sitting on a throne at the water's edge. Herodotus says that he had kind words for only one person, a woman. Queen Artemisia of Halicarnassus had come with her five warships to fight against the Greeks, "notwithstanding that she was a woman," says Herodotus. "She had now a son grown up, yet her brave spirit and manly daring sent her forth to the war, when no need required her to adventure. . . . the five triremes which she furnished to the Persians were, next to the Sidonian, the most famous ships in the fleet. She likewise gave to Xerxes sounder counsel than any of his other allies." When Xerxes saw that some of the best fighting on his side at Salamis was being done by Artemisia, he said, "My men have become women, and my women men."

After Salamis, Xerxes went home, taking a large part of his troops with him. But he left a sizable, well-trained force with Mardonius, with orders to retreat north into Thessaly for the winter and return to the attack in the spring. When Mardonius started south to renew the fight, the Greeks again fell into disagreement over the proper measures of defense. Athens asked for help from the Peloponnesian generals, who once more procrastinated, so that Athens once more had to threaten to withdraw from the war. Finally, after the cities of Megara and Plataea added their pleas to those of Athens, the generals acceded. While they had argued, the Persians had moved from Thessaly through Boeotia to the borders of Attica.

With a combined force of some 100,000 men under the Spartan general, Pausanias, the Greeks moved north, driving Mardonius back into Boeotia, where he took up a position near Plataea. The Greeks followed and encamped near him. Mardon-

VITAL NEW CREEDS

When the Persians first attacked mainland Greece in 492 B.C. the philosopher Confucius (above) was teaching in China. A dedicated reformer, he urged a return to the moral standards of an earlier epoch. His doctrine was one of several great creeds which arose almost simultaneously and won millions of followers in the East.

Persia itself, administering its territories and intermittently warring with the Greeks, was being converted to another new creed —Zoroastrianism. Based on the beliefs of the teacher Zoroaster, this esoteric religion outlasted the Persian Empire and gave wide currency to such momentous concepts as a day of judgment and the all-pervasive struggle between good and evil.

A third creed spreading at this time was born of the teachings of a semilegendary Chinese philosopher, Lao Tzu. Partly in reaction to the feudal wars that were disrupting China late in the Chou Dynasty, Lao Tzu taught that man's salvation lay in renouncing society and retiring into a life of solitary contemplation.

In India, where the great mass of the people found in their religion little but obscure ritual and the need for costly sacrifices, Gautama Buddha arose to offer them the comforts of a gentle philosophy of life ruled by compassion and self-denial.

ius waited for them to attack, planning to counter-attack with his cavalry and destroy them. In the meantime he hoped that the waiting would reveal cracks and dissensions in the Greek ranks. Both calculations were sound, and there were moments when both seemed likely to be realized. But the actual conflict, when it came, was almost accidental and its outcome, to Mardonius at least, was certainly unforeseen. Mardonius mistook a Greek shift of position for a retreat, and attacked, but Pausanias rallied his men and fought back with skill and courage. Mardonius himself was killed, his main infantry force was slaughtered; the rest of his army retreated northward as fast as it could.

On the very same day, according to Herodotus, the remainder of the Persian navy was also destroyed. Greek ships followed the Persians into the harbor of Mycale, on the coast of Asia Minor, where they had beached their ships. The Greeks went ashore, defeated the Persians and burned the Persian ships.

By any standards the victory of the Greeks over Persia was an astonishing achievement. No other people, faced with the full weight of Persian military strength, had done anything to equal it—and the Greeks had done it under handicaps. Only the Spartan forces were strictly professional; the rest of the Greek army, as well as the navy, was largely composed of ordinary citizens. Also, the Greeks had never arrived at a truly unified course of action. Although all the members of the League had a common aim, each put the interests of its own state first in matters of policy.

In view of the odds against them, it is not surprising that the Greeks were filled with pride, self-confidence and patriotism at their achievement, and that in their minds, their actions and their literature, the war assumed epic proportions. The dead were celebrated in noble epitaphs. Those who had not supported the Greek cause were regarded as mortal enemies. In 472 B.C. the dramatist Aeschylus departed from the usual tragic themes of Greek theater to honor the victors—and the new Greek spirit—in the majestic poetry of *The Persians:*

> *Behold this vengeance, and remember
> Greece,*
> *Remember Athens: henceforth let not
> pride,*
> *Her present state disdaining, strive to
> grasp*
> *Another's, and her treasured happiness*
> *Shed on the ground: such insolent
> attempts*
> *Awake the vengeance of offended Jove.*
> *But you, whose age demands more
> temperate thoughts,*
> *With words of well placed counsel teach
> his youth*
> *To curb that pride, which from the gods
> calls down*
> *Destruction on his head.*

But it was not contemporary Greeks alone who were stirred and inspired by the Greek victories. In the centuries that have passed since Marathon, Thermopylae and Salamis, the names of these epochal battles have become synonymous with man's unending quest to be free. Lord Byron, writing in the early 19th Century of a Greece then under another Asian power, the Ottoman Empire, put into one stanza the feelings evoked, more than two millennia later, by one of these battles:

> *The mountains look on Marathon—*
> *And Marathon looks on the sea;*
> *And musing there an hour alone,*
> *I dream'd that Greece might still be free;*
> *For standing on the Persians' grave,*
> *I could not deem myself a slave.*

A TENDER LOVE *that warmed many homes of classical Greece, despite the firm discipline, is shown in a grouping of grandmother and child. It is taken from a tombstone whose poignant inscription tells of the grandmother's happiness at having held the child.*

A ZEST FOR LIVING

In pleasure-loving Athens the routine of daily life was as simple as in stern and authoritarian Sparta, but the Athenians brought to their every activity a sense of excitement unparalleled elsewhere. Every day these zestful people were up with the sun and to their work. Philosophers paced walkways talking to students, unheeding the clatter of trade in the markets and trials in the law courts nearby. Like most Greeks the Athenians professed to love leisure—and in truth there was always time for good talk and, at the end of day, a rousing banquet—but it was a complaint elsewhere in Greece that the Athenians were "by nature incapable of either living a quiet life themselves or of allowing anyone else to do so."

FOR THE VERY YOUNG, *there was a two-wheeled cart to pull about, here shown in a vase painting. Besides these, there were also simple wheels attached to long poles that were "horses." Toys were sometimes homemade or the product of small shops.*

TOYS FOR BOYS *included terra-cotta figurines, like this one of a boy riding a goose, "destined for the beguiling of little children."*

TOYS FOR GIRLS *included dolls. Many Greek girls, who were married off as early as 14, often played with toys until their wedding day.*

THE GOLDEN YEARS OF GROWING UP

A Greek child grew up in an enchanting world—if he survived his first fortnight. For 10 days after birth the father could inspect the baby, and if he found it deformed or weak, he could order it to be exposed in some public place to die. Once he approved, the wonders appeared. In addition to the playthings shown on these pages, there were terra-cotta rattles with pebbles in them for tots. For older children, there were swings, seesaws, kites, balls and all manner of games. During the early years the mother was in charge. Her task was to provide a life free of sorrow, fear and pain in the first three years, and full of sports and amusement in the second three. Then the golden era ended. After their sixth birthday boys and girls were separated. The girls stayed at home with their mothers. The boys were sent to school to learn to be men.

ROLLING THE HOOP *was a favorite sport for boys in ancient Greece. Hoops, made of iron, often had bells and rings to make a glittering display and a tinkling sound as the hoop rolled.*

LONG SEASONS OF STRIVING FOR EXCELLENCE

After they left the freedom of the nursery, Athenian children were strictly reared. Plato recorded Protagoras' words: "Mother and nurse and father and tutor are vying with one another about the improvement of the child as soon as ever he is able to understand what is being said to him . . . If he obeys, well and good; if not, he is straightened by threats and blows, like a piece of bent or warped wood." From their seventh to 18th years, boys attended private schools, often under the guard of a slave. In daily classes, sometimes held in the open streets by harassed schoolmasters who were publicly disdained and often unpaid, students learned reading, writing, arithmetic, poetry and music. Paradoxically, these institutions came into existence because the law required parents to educate their sons but did not require the state to provide schools —and they became the best in the classical world.

A BOY FISHERMAN *is intently playing a fish that is nibbling on his line (right). He may have been playing hooky from the classroom, but an overflowing creel might well calm his displeased parents.*

IN THE CLASSROOM *two scholars (below), in front of their seated teachers, learn to play the pipes and to write. At the right sits the pedagogue, an elderly slave who brings the student to school.*

A SIMPLE MEAL, *such as might have been pre-pared by the wife of a humble Athenian 2,400 years ago, is displayed on the opposite page. The tableware and utensils date from the Fifth Century B.C. Spread out are leeks, olives, cheese, fish, bread, drinking mugs, flasks for oil and vinegar, and a stone grinder in a round bowl. High in the background is the Acropolis. Athenians usually ate little or no breakfast, a light lunch and then, in late afternoon, consumed a heavier dinner.*

THE QUIET LIVES
OF WIVES AND MOTHERS

Athenian society was organized pre-eminently as a man's world. Women were expected to prepare the meals, run their households—and stay out of sight. Fathers arranged marriages for their adolescent daughters. Thereafter, wives came under total control of their husbands. They received much male advice on the subject of staying home and being silent. The playwright Menander told them, "The loom is women's work and not debate." When their husbands entertained guests at dinner the women remained in their own quarters on the second floor, anointing their bodies with fragrant essences and sweet-scented oils, dreamily watching the street traffic through the windows. But husbands did not entertain every night, and when there were no guests man and wife shared each other's company. Thus the segregated relationship ordained by society melted into the family love that again and again is pictured in vase painting and sculpture.

A WOMAN WITH MIRROR, *shown at right, is inspecting her makeup. Among the various cosmetics used during this period were scents, white lead to whiten skin and alkanet root to redden the cheeks.*

WEAVING AT HOME, *two women at a loom (above) pass the shuttle. Most homes were small workshops, where household necessities were produced from raw materials.*

WORKING ON A STATUE, *an artist (below) colors a figure of Heracles with thick wax paint. Nearly all the sculpture of ancient Greece was originally painted.*

MEASURING *for a sandal, a shoemaker (below) places his customer's foot on the leather and cuts the sole. Indoors and in summer many Greeks went barefoot.*

IN A BUTCHER'S SHOP, *a boy holds a quarter of beef as the butcher (above) cuts. Meat was a luxury and it was seldom eaten, save on festive occasions.*

BUSY COMMERCE IN A CLASSICAL CITY

Athens bustled. Its marketplace, where odors of rare perfumes mingled with those of the day's catch of fish, swarmed with people. Its streets were full of little shops. The largest factory in the Greek world was probably Cephalus' arsenal, with 120 slaves, though there were mines which used more. But the average business was likely to employ not more than a half-dozen slaves, and in these shops free men and slaves worked together. Athenians of Per-

icles' day saw nothing despicable in work, providing that it did not demean the human spirit by limiting a man's freedom. The great Solon had required fathers to teach their sons a trade, and skilled artisans gloried in the name "lord of the hand"; monotonous toil, however, they considered fit only for the lower orders. Athenian craftsmen of course left their benches to attend the Assembly. But they were just as ready to stop whenever they were tired or bored.

THE GREEK PLOWMAN *was badly served by his simple plow (above).*
Despite its iron share and his own hard work, it scarcely turned
the earth. To finish up he had to put his back into swinging a pick.

A MERCHANT, *assisted by two boys (above), adds a little weight to*
bring his scales into balance. Besides his commodities the trader
overseas peddled an invisible export—Greece's language and culture.

MERCHANT SHIPS *had capacious hulls for cargo, steering oars and*
loading ladders (right). These vessels sailed only in favoring winds.
But roads were so few and so bad that ships offered the easiest travel.

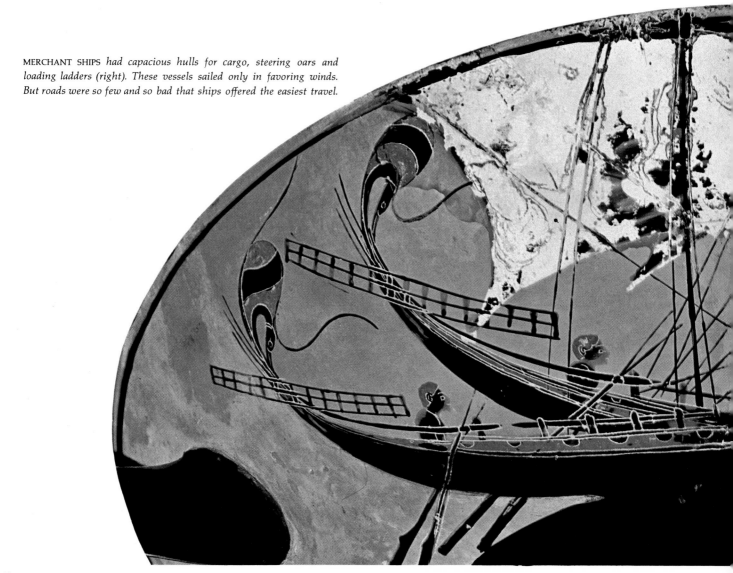

VITAL WORK ON LAND AND SEA

Greek agriculture changed little in the course of antiquity. Knowing nothing of crop rotation, the Greeks sowed their fields in one-year-harvest, next-year-fallow cycles. They persisted in reaping wheat with a sickle for want of a scythe and threshing grain by driving cattle over it, but they did learn how to drain swamps and terrace hillsides. Never was the Greek farmer able to feed all of Greece, but he produced things (wine and olive oil and wool) that, added to the manufacture of the cities (pottery and jewelry), could be traded all around the Mediterranean and Black Sea areas. Greek merchants wandered from the Crimea in the east to France and Ireland in the west. Besides the grains that were always needed, they brought back many good things: cheese and pork from Sicily, rugs from Carthage, ivory from Ethiopia, glass from Egypt and perfumes from far Araby.

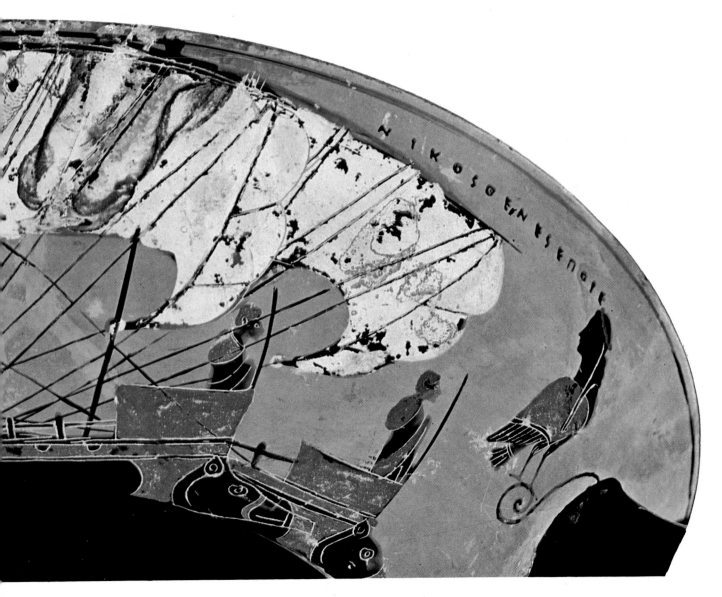

AT THE START OF A PARTY, *guests recline on couches, sing the Paean to Dionysus, giver of wine, and listen to a flute-girl play. Later the guests will sing more frivolous songs to the flute.*

AT THE END OF A PARTY, *a wine-laden husband comes home. He is hammering at the doorway with the butt end of his torch, while his young wife, lamp in hand, fearfully trembles within.*

AFTER THE DAY'S WORK—A BANQUET

At Athenian banquets, guests concentrated on the food; the sparkling conversations were a feature of the symposium, or drinking session that followed. Here the most important man was the symposiarch, chosen by lot or a throw of the dice, who took charge of everything. He decided how much water would be mixed with the wine, called in the enter-tainers—dancing girls, acrobats and magicians—and set the guests to entertaining one another. A symposiarch like the philosopher Socrates might pose brain-crunching riddles, but less intellectual symposiarchs would assign a bald-headed man to comb his hair, a stutterer to orate or an ardent fellow to race round the room with the flute-girl in his arms.

5

ATHENS IN ITS TIME OF GLORY

The great victory of the Greeks over the Persians left Sparta the most important power in Greece. In spite of its hesitations and shortcomings in the planning of the war, its troops had fought well and courageously. Athens, for all its fine showing at Marathon and Salamis, came off second best. And yet, for the next 50 years, Athens counted for almost everything in Greek life, and Sparta for almost nothing. From the retirement of the Persians in 479 B.C. until the outbreak of the Peloponnesian War in 431 B.C., Athens displayed a phenomenal vitality. This, in fact, was the Athenian Golden Age, without parallel in the history of man.

The major strength and inspiration for this development was Athens' democratic form of government, the first true democracy in history. In the most precise and literal sense of the word, the Athenians governed themselves. The process begun by Cleisthenes in 507 B.C. with constitutional reforms was completed by Ephialtes in 462-461 B.C. Ephialtes stripped the aristocrats of all their powers except for certain judicial functions in matters of homicide, and certain religious duties. For this act the nobles murdered Ephialtes, but his democracy survived. Thereafter, no political body stood above the popular Assembly.

The Athenian Assembly was open to all free male citizens of adult age, regardless of income or class. It met 40 times a year, usually at a place called the Pnyx, a natural amphitheater on one of the hills west of the Acropolis. In theory, any member of the Assembly could speak about anything, providing he could command an audience. But for practical reasons, there was also an official agenda. This was prepared by a Council composed of 500 men, 50 from each of the 10 Attic tribes. They were chosen by lot from a list of volunteers, all of them citizens over the age of 30. The Council was in no way a check on the Assembly; it simply made its deliberations easier. Council members were always paid for their services and served for a year. After an interval they might serve a second year, but they could never serve for more than two.

Within the Council was a smaller, inner council of 50 men, called the Prytany, which met every day and in effect administered the government. The composition of the Prytany changed 10 times a

A DOORWAY DOWN THE CENTURIES *is set in the walls of the Parthenon. Through the doorway may be seen the section of modern Athens in which is located the Agora of classical times. In the distance are the Attic hills.*

year, and its chairmanship, the chief executive position of Athens, changed every day. In theory no one man remained in power long enough to entrench himself. But in reality this opportunity was open to one class of men: the 10 generals of the armed forces who were elected directly from the Assembly and served for a year's term. A general could be re-elected any number of times. Inevitably the generals played a large and sometimes continuing role in nonmilitary affairs.

Unlike representative democracies or republics, in which one man is elected to speak for many, Athens was a true democracy: every citizen spoke for himself. Such a system of government can only exist when a population is small and intensely civic-minded, and Athens met both these conditions. Every Athenian citizen had the right to participate in the public life of his city, and it logically followed that he should have a voice in its government. But there was another reason why Athens could afford to be a true democracy. Ironically, that reason was slavery. With slaves to handle the daily domestic chores and the routine work of commerce and manufacturing, Athenian citizens were free to give their time to public affairs. They could not only attend and vote in the Assembly, but also assume public posts from time to time.

It has been estimated that the slave population of Attica around 430 B.C. was about 115,000 in a total population of 315,000. A rich mine contractor might employ as many as 1,000 slaves in several mines, and the largest household, about 20. Athenian slaves were born of other slaves, or acquired by piracy, or bought as captives taken in war. Many of them were not of Greek origin. They had, of course, no political rights, but their lot in general was no worse and sometimes it was better than that of slaves in other parts of the ancient world. The life of a slave who worked in the mines, where conditions were most unhealthy, was wretched

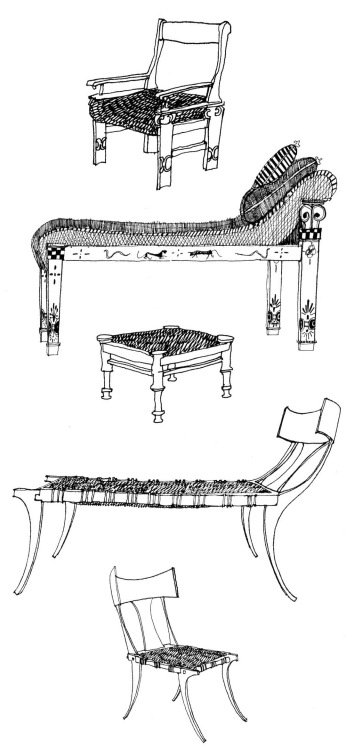

SPARSE, SIMPLE FURNITURE *graced Greek homes. Little of it has survived, but drawings such as those above can be made from vase paintings. The throne (top) was a seat of honor on state occasions. Just below, separated by a stool, are couches used both for sleeping and reclining at meals. The armless chair, or klismos (bottom), was the common seating place. Chair and couch seats were made of leather or fiber cords, on top of which cushions were placed. The Greeks also had chests and three-legged dining tables.*

indeed, but slaves sometimes received wages, as well as their keep, and sometimes their owners freed them. A few Athenians of independent mind recognized that slavery was in itself bad. One was the playwright Euripides, who wrote:

> Slavery,
> That thing of evil, by its nature evil,
> Forcing submission from man to what
> No man should yield to.

Aristotle, a century later, attempted to justify slavery by claiming that certain men became slaves because of their natural disposition to be servile. He failed to explain, however, why all servile men did not eventually become slaves.

A second group of underprivileged people in Athens was women. In the aristocratic age women had mixed freely with men, taking part in many public functions, although not in government. In Periclean Athens, however, a woman's place was theoretically in the home, and her main social obligation was to keep silent. No less a man than Pericles advised women that they should aspire to be anonymous: ". . . the greatest glory of a woman is to be least talked about by men, whether they are praising you or criticizing you." But theory does not seem to have jibed with practice and there is evidence of the facts being quite otherwise. Athenian drama, both tragedy and comedy, frequently gives women a place of major importance in the dramatic action. Antigone, in Sophocles' play about her, motivates the entire action by insisting on giving her brother a proper burial in defiance of temporal authority. And Lysistrata, in Aristophanes' comedy, uses a thoroughly feminine tactic to force Athens and Sparta to make peace.

If women could be assigned roles of such stature in the world of imagination, there is some argument for thinking that they must have enjoyed a degree of importance in the real world. Attic gravestones and funeral vases, in fact, portray scenes of domestic life that are touching and noble, and strongly suggest that Athenian marriage had much more to it than the provision of food and children. Public life may have been off bounds to a woman, but within her home she was far more than a servant. As the head of an operation which in some respects resembled a factory, a wife had a position of considerable responsibility. The home itself was physically simple—austerely furnished and uncomplicated in design—but almost everything that an Athenian family ate and wore was produced at home, under the wife's supervision. On rare occasions a woman's position was even more influential than this. Aspasia, the mistress of Pericles, is said to have helped Pericles to write his speeches, and her home was a center of Athenian intellectual life. Pericles loved her enough to divorce his wife for her, and thereafter, according to the later writer Plutarch, "every day, both as he went out and as he came in from the marketplace, he saluted and kissed her."

Having discovered the meaning and advantages of liberty and democracy, the Athenians had a passionate desire to impart their discoveries to others. In fact they saw themselves as charged with an exalted mission to do so, and the situation in Greece after the Persian retreat gave them excellent opportunities. Despite Sparta's enormous prestige, resulting from its wartime successes, that city played only a minor part in Greek political life. From a first feeble attempt at political leadership, the city's rulers quickly fell to quarreling internally—aristocrats against ambitious kings. Finally Sparta confined itself to a kind of isolationism, devoting its energies exclusively to maintaining the Spartan domain in the Peloponnesus.

This left Athens free to take over the leadership of Greece, and it moved to do so. During the winter

A FABULIST AND HIS FOX *chat in a drawing on the bottom of a cup. This is Aesop, a onetime slave who, legend says, wrote the famous fables. But today scholars doubt that Aesop ever lived.*

of 478-477 B.C. it proposed the formation of a league of Greek states for the purpose of harrying the Persians and protecting themselves from Persian reprisals. The Delian League, as it came to be called, included the Greek cities of Asia Minor, most of the Aegean islands, some towns on the Propontis and in Thrace, and most of the island of Euboea—in other words, most of the Greek states in or about the Aegean. It numbered at its height somewhere between 250 and 300 members.

Each member of the League agreed to contribute ships, if it was rich enough to do so, or, if it was not, money toward the building of ships which Athens would provide. The amount of this contribution was fixed according to each member's resources by Aristides, whose fairness caused him to become widely known as "Aristides the Just." At one performance of Aeschylus' play *Seven against Thebes*, the line, "modest and just and good and reverent" was taken by the audience to refer to him, and at its recital they broke into cheers.

The League's treasury was kept on the sacred island of Delos, site of a major shrine to Apollo. Delos was also the meeting place for the League's council. Each member had an equal voice in this council, but right from the beginning Athens dominated. It was willing to shoulder the heaviest burdens, and the allies were willing to have it so. Athens was thus, to all intents and purposes, mistress of the Aegean.

With the League for support, Athens soon renewed the offensive against Persia. Under Cimon, son of Miltiades, it liberated the provinces of Caria and Lycia on the southern coast of Asia Minor and brought them into the League. In about 468 B.C. it destroyed the new Persian fleet as it lay at anchor in the Eurymedon River, a fleet which Xerxes had built for a fresh invasion of the Aegean. This important victory not only justified the League's existence; it convinced Athens of the need to keep it

strong and united. Accordingly Athens thought that any state which benefited from the League ought to belong to it, and that any state which threatened to leave the League was guilty of treachery. When, earlier, the city of Carystus, on Euboea, refused to join, it had been attacked and forced to do so. And when the islands of Naxos and Thasos tried to leave, Athens not only compelled them to stay in, but punished them by making them tributary states. The threat of secession could indeed be considered a disloyal act, a breach of a solemn pledge. But the real reason for Athens' punitive measures was a belief in the value of the League to Athens itself, quite apart from its original value as a military alliance.

Ultimately, Athens' dominance of the League resulted in its becoming the ruler of the League. States which contributed ships continued to rank as equals, but in time, there were only three of these: Chios, Lesbos and Samos. The rest paid tribute and were reduced to a lower station. They often found their affairs managed by Athenian officials supported by an Athenian garrison, and in addition to paying tribute, had to contribute soldiers. Athens claimed final jurisdiction over all criminal cases—even in those states ostensibly its equals. It also reserved the right to settle any matter, such as conspiracy or treason, that threatened the safety of the League. In 454-453 B.C. it insisted on transferring the League treasury from Delos to Athens, where it was completely at the disposal of the Athenians. Finally, it demanded that all the allies use Athenian coinage and the Athenian system of weights and measures.

In all this, there was some reason, and even some advantage to the League members. An Athenian garrison might protect some outlying state from hostile raids or civil disorders. A central court meant that certain legal policies were identical for all states. A single coinage was of obvious advantage in commerce. In fact, the Athenian coins, stamped with the head of Athena on one side and her owl on the other, were the most respected of currencies throughout the eastern Mediterranean. Finally, the treasury was certainly far safer in Athens than on the vulnerable island of Delos. Clearly, however, the League was no longer a confederacy, but an empire ruled from Athens.

In ruling that empire, Athens claimed to be looking after its allies' welfare and safety, and in fact it frequently was. As long as the Athenian fleet was maintained at a high level of preparedness and efficiency, the Athenian Empire was safe from Persian attack, as the victory at the Eurymedon had so triumphantly showed. It was also safe from pirates, the immemorial pests of the Aegean, many of whom were now eliminated (their stronghold on the rocky island of Scyros, for instance, was cleared in 474-473 B.C.).

Furthermore, in interfering with the internal arrangements of its allies, Athens in many cases established a democratic government not unlike its own. The dispossessed aristocrats complained bitterly and were a potential source of trouble, but the majority of the people were probably better off po-

litically than before. This bound them to Athens, despite their wounded pride at being deprived of their local independence. Also they knew that if Athens relinquished control and the local aristocrats regained their power, they would exact a bloody revenge. This more than anything else probably accounts for the remarkable loyalty to the Empire. Even when it might have been safe to throw off the Athenian yoke, few did.

For a while, after the Empire was formed, the Athenians seemed to have felt that nothing could withstand them. Their ships made them masters of the Aegean and the coasts beyond. Trade prospered and gave them sufficient resources, both financial and industrial, to wage war on an extensive scale. In 459 B.C. they incorporated the neighboring state of Megara into the Empire at its own request, and dispatched a large expedition to Egypt in support of a local Egyptian king who had rebelled against the Persians. In 458 B.C. they attacked Aegina and, after two years, captured it, compelling it to join the League. In 457 B.C. they conquered all of Boeotia except Thebes. Some inkling of the multiplicity of Athenian enterprises can be gotten from a memorial, raised during this period, recording the names of citizens from a single tribe who fell in battle during one year, 459-458 B.C., "In Cyprus, in Egypt, in Phoenicia, at Halieis, in Aegina, at Megara."

This policy of aggression was not entirely successful, but considering the number of fronts, the marvel is that it was successful at all. The Egyptian campaign against Persia lasted for some six years and ended in complete disaster, with the surrender of the Egyptians and their Athenian allies, and the destruction of their ships. Boeotia was held for 10 years, and then lost. Athens would certainly have come to ruin if it had continued this policy, even though its gains remained substantial. Fortunately, after a decade of aggression it settled down to con-

solidate its winnings and see what other kinds of activity lay open to it.

This ensuing period is associated with the name of Pericles, who more than any other man embodies the spirit of Athens in its heyday. An aristocrat from a traditionally pro-democratic family (the constitutional reformer Cleisthenes was his great-uncle), Pericles had a philosophy that embraced both democracy and empire. Personally aloof, choosing his friends from the leading thinkers of his day, he was nevertheless popular with many men. He owed his position of influence to his ability in the Assembly, where he was a most effective speaker and a coiner of memorable phrases. He called Aegina, for instance, "the eyesore of the Piraeus," and in a funeral oration for the dead of the Peloponnesian War said that "The city has lost its youth; it is as though the year had lost its spring." But what truly won Pericles the Assembly's trust was his foresight and initiative in planning Athenian policy. In time Pericles actually came to lead the democracy, even though officially he remained an annually elected general.

Pericles had a dream for Athens. By 443 B.C. his main opponents were discredited and he was free to pursue it. He proposed to make Athens a great city in more than one sense of the word. He was not an advocate of wide expansion on the mainland, having tried this unsuccessfully, but he was determined to enlarge the maritime empire, and he encouraged alliances favorable to trade on the farther fringes of the Greek world. In fact Pericles himself visited the Black Sea for this purpose, in command of an imposing squadron.

He also believed that the glory of Athens should be revealed in visible form. It is to his inspiration, insight and powers of persuasion that we owe the great buildings on the Acropolis, whose substantial remains are evocations of their grandeur in Pericles' time. In 480 B.C. the Persians had com-

RECORD OF SALE

ALLOTMENT TOKENS

OSTRACISM BALLOT

pletely devastated the Acropolis, and the Athenians had subsequently incorporated the debris from its temples and statues into the city's rebuilt foundations and its new walls. So Pericles began from scratch. He employed the very best architects and artists of his time, and gave the project his own unflagging support by persuading the Assembly to make annual grants of money for the cost.

The Propylaea was the great gateway to the holy places of the Acropolis, functioning also as an art gallery and public meeting place; its stern majesty dominated, and still dominates, the entrance. Its style, with its unusual mixture of Doric and Ionic columns, catches the very spirit of Athens—strength tempered by grace. Like the Parthenon it is made of a local marble, quarried from Mount Pentelicus near Athens, which changes its color with the changing light, varying from gold and honey to rose and gray.

The radiantly beautiful Parthenon was the spiritual center of Athens. Unlike some Greek temples, it served only one divinity, the goddess Athena, spirit of creative and active intelligence and the guardian deity of Athens. The whole plan was subordinated to her worship. The Parthenon was begun in 447 B.C. and finished in 432 B.C. Its architect was Ictinus, its "master of works" Callicrates, and its decorations were designed and supervised by the sculptor Phidias. It is one of the largest known Greek temples, and although its main outlines are simple, the simplicity is carefully contrived. Many ingenious adaptations make lines look straight or tapering when in fact they are neither. Standing on its hill it is visible from miles around, especially from the sea—ships crossing the Saronic Gulf saw it from afar, the manifest evidence of Athenian wealth and power.

For Athenians, however, the Parthenon was much more than this. It was a sacred shrine as well as symbol of temporal authority. Standing inside in the shadowy sanctuary was Phidias' monumental statue of Athena, 40 feet high, fashioned of wood and covered in gold and ivory—gold for the goddess' clothing, ivory for her flesh. But the statue no longer exists. It was carried off to Constantinople in the late Fifth Century A.D., where it was destroyed by fire sometime between the Sixth Century and 10th Century A.D. The only record of it that remains is its image on coins and gems, in metalwork and in later, smaller copies in marble.

A large part of the sculpture from the exterior of the building does survive, however—the pediments, most of the frieze and a number of the metopes (originally there were 92). Phidias cannot possibly have done it all, but it is done in his style and is obviously of his design. The metopes portray various conflicts between men and their enemies, for instance the Centaurs, half-man, half-horse, whose defeat signifies the triumph of order over barbarism. The frieze encircling the building depicts the colorful procession climaxing Athena's festival, the Great Panathenaea, held every fourth year. It is a solemn and also a happy occasion, a holy day and a holiday. Every kind of creature—human and animal, young and old, men and women and children, horses and cattle and sheep—is shown taking part in it. All of them are distinctly themselves, infinitely varied and individual, but each one is also caught up in the spirit of a magnificent celebration, mindful of the presence of watchful and friendly gods.

At either end of the temple the huge triangular pediments were filled with sculptures. At the eastern end the birth of Athena, goddess of wisdom and intelligence, expresses what the emergence of so marvelous a power meant to the dreaming gods of Olympus. At the western end, the struggle between Athena and the sea god Poseidon for supremacy symbolizes the goddess' successful domination of the city's religious life, and the city's domination

PERICLES ON DEMOCRACY

In the winter of 431-430 B.C., with the Peloponnesian War begun, Pericles made his funeral oration. Instead of praising only the dead, he chose to extol Athens. Below are two stirring passages translated by the scholar Rex Warner.

"Our constitution is called a democracy because power is in the hands not of a minority but of the whole people. When it is a question of settling private disputes, everyone is equal before the law; when it is a question of putting one person before another in positions of public responsibility, what counts is not membership of a particular class, but the actual ability which the man possesses."

"Here each individual is interested not only in his own affairs but in the affairs of the state as well . . . we do not say that a man who takes no interest in politics is a man who minds his own business; we say that he has no business here at all. . . . And this is another point where we differ from other people. We are capable at the same time of taking risks and of estimating them beforehand. Others are brave out of ignorance; and, when they stop to think, they begin to fear. But the man who can most truly be accounted brave is he who best knows the meaning of what is sweet in life and of what is terrible, and then goes out undeterred to meet what is to come."

of the sea, cradle and grave-to-be of its glories.

The sculptures of the Parthenon are the incomparable peak of Greek art. Nearly 20 years earlier, in the great metopes and pediments of the temple of Zeus at Olympia, gifted artists had freed themselves from the limitations of archaic art and achieved the effect of life and action through their intimate knowledge of the human body. But the art of the Parthenon is altogether a finer, more varied achievement. The sculptures are set high on the building, well above eye level, and yet nothing is skimped in their execution. The backs of the great figures on the pediments are as firmly and delicately carved as the fronts. And though each sculpture has a dominant pattern, relating it to the central composition, even the smallest detail is worked out with a sensitive appreciation for the revealing stroke. Invention, originality and variety are everywhere present, but there is not a single trace of surprise for surprise's sake, or of ingenuity reduced to the merely ingenious. The sculptures of the Parthenon, combining the old aristocratic appreciation for fine craftsmanship with the vigor and confidence of the new democracy, are the essence of Periclean Athens. For a few brief years a perfect equilibrium existed between the old and the new—and the genius of Phidias, supported by Pericles, gave it visible form.

The lofty vision embodied in the Parthenon's sculpture was matched by the development of a no less lofty poetry. The chief form of this was tragic drama, but Greek tragedy differed from modern tragedy in many ways. To begin with, it was a religious rite, performed at annual festivals in the Theater of Dionysus for the whole population. Its theme was the relationship between men and the gods, and its plot, usually drawn from heroic myth, illustrated some particular problem or lesson. But the profundity of its purpose did not exclude sharp delineation of character or intense dramatic moments. The plays themselves were short, although sometimes trilogies were performed and people spent whole days in the theater. A large part of the performance was devoted to the chorus, which commented on the action at intervals throughout the drama. The actors wore masks, often representing the character's mood as well as his role.

There were three great masters of Greek tragedy in the Fifth Century B.C. whose work has survived in part—Aeschylus, Sophocles and Euripides. All three wrote plays for the Dionysiac and Lenaean festivals, but they differed markedly from each other. Aeschylus, the poet who best evokes Athenian power and grandeur, is deeply concerned with the moral issues that power and grandeur raise. He examines the dangers of overweening arrogance, the ancient rule of blood for blood, the inevitability of the misuse of power. His conclusions are his own, often breaking with traditional concepts. His characters are recognizable human individuals even though they move in a theatrical world of uninhibited passions, personal magnificence and unfailing splendor of speech.

Among the most memorable of Aeschylus' plays are the three concerned with the story of Orestes, son of Agamemnon, the conqueror of Troy. The trilogy—*Agamemnon*, *Choephoroe* and *Eumenides* —tells the story of Orestes' murder of his mother, Clytaemnestra, for her murder of his father. For his crime Orestes is pursued by the Furies until Athena, taking pity on him, prevails upon the Furies to become Eumenides—Kindly Ones—and serve her as subsidiary goddesses.

Sophocles works in a different way. Where Aeschylus argues for and justifies the ways of the gods, Sophocles is content to accept them as they are, and treats them with awe and reverence. He examines the accepted view of some problem and from it draws its central truth. To Sophocles, any violation of the cosmic order creates suffering, but suffering can redeem and exalt. His power lies in his compassion, in his sympathy for his characters, however deluded or broken they may be. One of the best examples of this is his treatment of Oedipus in *Oedipus Rex*. Sophocles makes him a good-hearted but headstrong young man who kills his own father without knowing that he is his father, and marries his mother without realizing that she is his mother. When he discovers what he has done, he blinds himself in a paroxysm of horror and remorse.

Euripides, the last of the three great tragedians, belongs to a somewhat later generation of Greek thought, and is a far more troubled, questioning and unsatisfied spirit. He comes to no clear conclusions and is a less certain craftsman, but he has moments of astonishing insight into human character. Sophocles reportedly said of him that, "He paints men as they are," and of himself, "I paint men as they ought to be." Euripides is also the most direct of the three in his questioning of established beliefs. Where Aeschylus and Sophocles merely suggest that the old ways may be wrong, Euripides criticizes them boldly. And yet, skeptic though he is, he treats passion and grief with moving lyricism. In *The Trojan Women*, Andromache, the Trojan princess, relinquishes her small son to be killed by the Greeks with these words:

"Thou little thing
That curlest in my arms, what sweet
   scents cling
All round thy neck! Beloved; can it be
All nothing, that this bosom cradled thee
And fostered; all the weary nights where-
   through
I watched upon thy sickness, till I grew
Wasted with watching? Kiss me. This
   one time;
Not ever again. Put up thine arms, and
   climb

About my neck: now, kiss me, lips to
    lips. . . .
O, ye have found an anguish that out-
    strips
All tortures of the East, ye gentle Greeks!"

Greek tragedy is not tragic in one modern sense —it does not always end unhappily. Sometimes it ends with the healing of wounds and the restoration of harmony to a broken world. But it is intensely and relentlessly serious. It can be wry and ironic, but never purely comic. There are no moments of lowered tension—everything is played at the highest pitch. Even if there is a happy end, everything that precedes it is dark and anxious. It presents man's position before the gods as uncertain, fragile and dangerous—and the gods as inescapable, never far away.

Christianity has alleviated much of the tragic view of life which was implicit in Greek thought— the assumption that the gods were inscrutable and inexorable in their dealings with men. But modern thought still retains the Greek belief that man's acceptance of his fate, no matter how intolerable that fate may seem, can be ennobling. Greek tragedy provides no explicit answers for the sufferings of humanity, but it exposes them and shows how they happen, and how they may be borne.

Attic comedy, in every other respect the antithesis of tragedy, also had a religious origin and was also performed at a festival of Dionysus. Where tragedy offered release from life's mysteries in pity and understanding, comedy offered the release of heart-easing ridicule and rollicking mirth. Its practitioners were restrained by laws neither of libel nor obscenity, and two of its early masters, Cratinus and Eupolis, both largely concerned with politics, were uninhibited caricaturists. But the greatest of the writers of Attic comedy was Aristophanes, who made fun equally of politicians, generals, phi-

losophers, scientists, poets and prominent citizens —and whose fun is ribald, audacious, indecent, reckless and, above all, imaginative.

Aristophanes' situations are brilliantly absurd, and his characters, taken straight from life, burst with vitality. His choral lyrics are winged with the very spirit of song. Even at his funniest, however, Aristophanes had serious intentions, and was not afraid of expressing them. He wrote after the death of Pericles, when the shadows were deepening for Athens. He ridicules public affairs and does so freely, but he also puts forward intelligent ideas about uniting the Athenian Empire or coming to terms with Sparta. Yet he does it without solemnity, packing his messages between riotous jokes and scandalous malice.

If Greek tragedy shows the Athenians' depth of thought on the fundamental issues of life and death, Greek comedy shows their ability to face almost any situation with lightheartedness. They were never afraid of the truth, no matter how undignified or disreputable it was, and this was an incalculable asset. It helps to explain why the Athenians were able to hold their own for so long, even when their star was declining. Part of their strength indubitably was their ability to laugh at themselves.

Because Periclean Athens was the intellectual center of Greece, it naturally drew from other cities men who knew that their intellectual gifts would be welcomed and honored there. Among them was Anaxagoras of Clazomenae, a personal friend of Pericles. Anaxagoras had an interesting theory about the universe. He believed that it was an organized system of matter, comparable to a living organism, and that the force which moved it was a mental process similar to that of the mind. It was also in Athens that the views of the philosopher Democritus of Abdera slowly found recognition. His atomic theory differs in every detail from modern theories, but does at least use similar terminology: it says that the primary substance of things consists of indivisible units it calls atoms.

Among the greatest of these Athenian visitors was Herodotus of Halicarnassus. Herodotus was the "father of history," author of the great book on the Persian Wars. To collect information for it he traveled widely through the Greek world and into Egypt, Babylonia, Syria and southern Scythia. Everywhere he asked questions and noted the answers. Herodotus' sympathies are with Athens but he is remarkably fair, and even generous, to the Persians. He sees the whole war as an epic event, larger than life, but at the same time he is concerned with its actual participants and its factual background. He includes details on many matters which caught his interest but are not immediately related to the war, and on past events that happened outside Greece, notably in Asia and Egypt. He is also deeply interested in personalities, in individual men, and he writes of them with a delighted observation that makes him the father, not just of history, but of other social sciences too.

Herodotus did his best to discover the truth. Sometimes he failed, or got it wrong, but the lapses are minor compared to the thoroughness of his effort. Many times he gives firsthand information from actual witnesses, or gives both sides of a story, leaving the reader to make up his own mind. He writes with great force, humor, sympathy and liveliness. In style and spirit he blends Ionia with Athens; he treats history as both an art and a science, on one side recalling the poetic spirit of Homer, on the other invoking the scientific temper of his age.

During this same period medicine also developed into a science. The development is associated with Hippocrates of Cos, the first and most famous of a group of physicians who formed a school of medicine, in the sense that they adhered to a common medical doctrine. They followed common practices, accepted a common body of knowledge, exchanged

ETHICS OF MEDICINE

A grateful patient (above) brings a replica of his cured leg to the shrine of Asclepius, god of healing. Hippocrates, to whom is attributed the oath for new doctors printed in part below, was considered the ideal physician of his time —one who sought cures in science, not in gods.

I swear by Apollo . . . to reckon him who taught me this art equally dear to me as my parents . . . I will impart a knowledge of the art to my own sons, and those of my teachers . . . I will give no deadly medicine to any one if asked nor suggest any such counsel . . . Into whatever houses I enter, I will go into them for the benefit of the sick, and will abstain from every voluntary act of mischief . . . Whatever . . . I see or hear, in the life of men . . . I will not divulge . . .

ideas with one another, developed new theories from established discoveries and worked strictly on scientific principles. Hippocrates stressed the importance of careful observation and classification, and believed that it was impossible to understand a part of the human body without understanding the whole. With this knowledge, said Hippocrates, a doctor could proceed to diagnosis, and diagnosis was the central point of Hippocratic doctrine.

The science of medicine affected all thought in the Fifth Century. When Herodotus' great successor, Thucydides, wrote *The Peloponnesian War*, he examined the causes of the war in an almost clinical spirit. Like a good scientist, Thucydides was determined to find the truth. He believed that the experiences of one generation were relevant to those of another, and that later generations could therefore learn from their predecessors. Consequently he often stopped to analyze a specific occurrence in terms of its application to a more general problem. Although his conception of history is almost purely political, largely lacking in Herodotus' concern with human personalities, Thucydides in his own way is extremely perceptive. Also, he is not afraid to draw moral conclusions. No one has better described the corruption of standards that comes from civil strife. No one has delineated more clearly the pitfalls of unrestrained power. And for all his self-control, Thucydides tells the story of an event with a full sense of its drama: its risks, its ugliness, its elements of tragedy. If his language is sometimes complicated, it is not intentionally so. He is serious, and he tries to state his thoughts exactly, including the emotion which colors them. Not until modern times has any historian shown a respect for truth so powerful and dominating, and very few historians of any time have treated events with so passionate a regard for what they mean in the lives of men.

As a result of this explosion of energy and power, Athens had become, by 460 B.C., an object of fear and alarm to other Greek states. They saw Athens busily extending its empire, often at the expense of unwilling victims, and at the same time promoting democracy with missionary zeal, a development that aristocratic governments viewed with shocked disapproval. This anti-Athenian point of view is expressed in the work of the poet Pindar of Thebes, whose patrons were rich aristocrats and tyrants. Aegina, where Pindar had many friends, and Boeotia, his native land, had both suffered from Athens' compulsive expansion. Consequently, although Pindar had begun by being well disposed to Athens, he ended by regarding its actions with distrust and disapproval. He criticized the Athenian spirit for destroying the sense of inner peace which was one of the chief blessings of life. He saw the city as an example of that self-pride which breeds its own ruin. Athens, he said, was like Bellerophon, who tried to scale the sky on the winged horse, Pegasus. It was like the Giants, who revolted against the gods, and were routed by them.

Like Pindar, many Greeks were troubled by Athens' insatiable activity, its unexpected interference in distant places, its refusal to leave things as they were. The Greek aristocrats deeply resented the emergence of a power which was likely to deprive them of their own power and privilege. But they resented no less the Athenian state of mind, which seemed to them the antithesis of their own. They were willing to let Athens go its own way if it would only let them go theirs, but this, they feared, it was not prepared to do. Fearing what Athens stood for, they failed completely to compete with it in the wide scope of its achievements. Neither in the fine arts nor in science did the established aristocracies begin to rival Athens. Indeed they seemed rather to have stuck where they were, and avoided new developments. Inevitably, a conflict in the two positions was bound to come, and when it came, it was the long and deadly Peloponnesian War.

THE CITY'S FIRST CITIZEN, *austere aristocrat, soldier, orator and statesman, was Pericles, shown above in his war helmet. He dominated the affairs of the city, cultural center of Greece, from 460 until 429 B.C.*

THE PERICLEAN EPOCH

Greece's Golden Age glowed brightest in Athens for the 30 years it had the leadership of the political genius whose bust is shown above. His city, of some 150,000 inhabitants, had two cores. One was made up of the great marketplace called the Agora and adjacent Pnyx Hill. The center of trade, schools and law courts, the Agora also harbored the offices of the world's first democratic government; the Assembly met on Pnyx Hill. The second core was the grouping of marbled temples, among them buildings the world has ever since counted its most beautiful, on top of the Acropolis, a rocky hill which was the heart of the city. The two Athenses—the city of creativity below and the one of beauty on the heights—made sober fact of Pericles' boast: "Our city is an education to Greece."

THE CITY OF PERICLES

The drawing on these pages shows the Athens Pericles built or helped plan. Rising above the rest of the city is the rocky Acropolis, with the structures whose ruins still inspire men: the Parthenon, the Propylaea, the temple of Athena Nike and the Erechtheum. Originally the Acropolis constituted the entire

fortified city, but it spread down into the valleys. Destroyed in war, it was rebuilt. Great walls enclosed it. In the Agora stood stoas, or open-sided markets, where the philosophers taught; the Bouleuterion, where the 500-man council met; the mint; courts; and the Strategeion, or military headquarters.

1. Unfinished Temple of Zeus
2. Unfinished law courts
3. Painted Stoa
4. Stoa of the Herms
5. Altar of the Twelve Gods
6. Stoa of Zeus with his statue
7. Temple of Hephaestus
8. Bouleuterion
9. Monument of the Eponymous Heroes
10. Tholos (administrative headquarters)
11. Strategeion
12. Southwest Fountain House
13. Heliaia law courts
14. South Stoa
15. Southeast Fountain House
16. Mint
17. Panathenaic festival procession
18. Pnyx
19. Areopagus
20. Temple of Athena Nike
21. Propylaea
22. Statue of Athena Promachos
23. Erechtheum
24. Parthenon

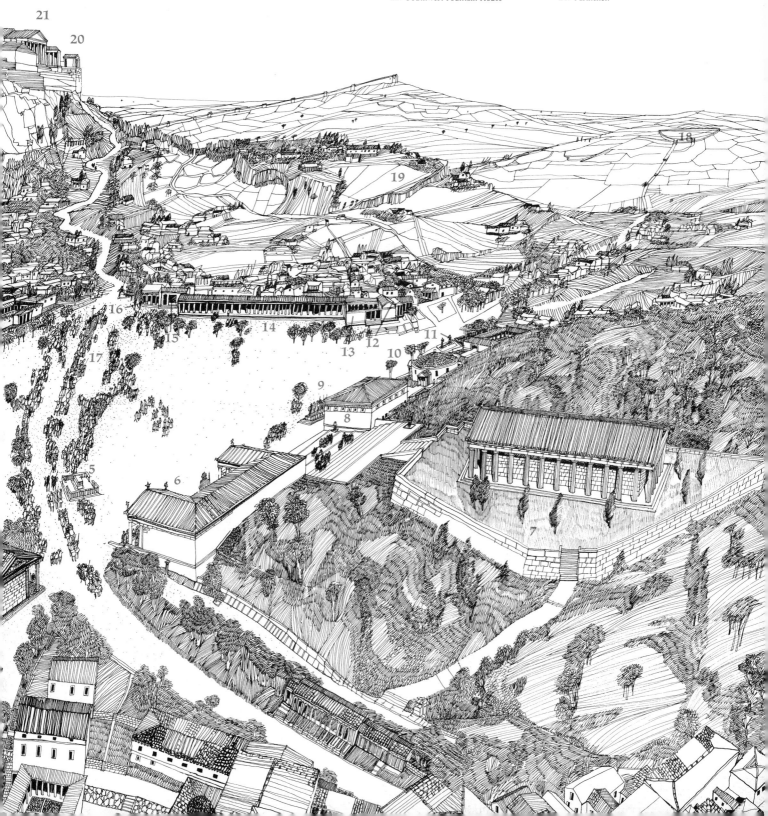

THE SPEAKER'S PODIUM *on Pnyx Hill faced a natural hillside amphitheater that seated 18,000. To ensure adequate attendance at a dull Assembly meeting, police with long ropes dipped in wet paint herded citizens to Pnyx Hill.*

AN EARLY ROSTRUM OF DEMOCRACY

Athens was a talkative town. It was ruled by its orators; Pericles became its leader because he was the best orator. All major decisions were reached by the Ecclesia, or Assembly of all citizens, which usually met about 40 times a year in the amphitheater dominated by the rostrum shown above. In addition, there was the Boule, a 500-man council chosen by lot. The Boule met daily, with a subcommittee available day and night, making decisions that were pressing and preparing the agenda for the Ecclesia. Among decisions reached in the Assembly during the golden era: to pay fees for public service, thus making office-holding possible for the poor; to reconstruct temples destroyed by Persians; and the fateful decision to fight Sparta.

A "KLEROTERION" *was used to select jurors. Slots in the device, a fragment of which is seen above, held individual volunteers' names. Black and white balls were dropped down a tube (not shown) to select jurors by groups.*

ORATING HORSEMAN, *like most Athenians a man of strong mind, gives the crowd a few words while waiting to ride in procession to the Acropolis.*

SHRINE TO THE BEGINNINGS OF A GREAT CITY

Wishing to enclose in splendor the sacred sites of the fables concerning the beginnings of Athens, the city architects produced the Erechtheum. It is on the north side of the Acropolis, where once stood what Homer called "the strong house of Erechtheus," a legendary king. Under a corner of the Erechtheum is the tomb of Cecrops, mythical first King of Athens. The building contained the gifts that the gods Poseidon and Athena gave the city in a contest to win its devotion. There were the marks of the fiery trident which Poseidon used to strike open a well of sea water, and the well itself. In a courtyard was the gnarled first olive tree of all time, which Athena gave the city and thereby won both the contest and the hearts of all true Athenians. Legend says the tree, destroyed by the Persians, sprang to life again after they left. To encompass all of these things the Erechtheum became a most unusual temple in this land of rectangular temples. It is not symmetrical; it is built on two levels; its porches, one of which is shown at left, bear no relation to one another. Yet it breathes Ionic grace and charm.

PORCH OF THE MAIDENS *on the Erechtheum has four original columns. The background figure has a modern head; the second from left in front is a cast of the original, now in the British Museum.*

IN PANATHENAIC PROCESSION, *paraders en route to the Acropolis carry jars of water, perhaps for sacrificial gifts. Their goal was the wooden statue of Athena that was housed in the Erechtheum.*

ATHENA'S TEMPLE

Three mighty talents collaborated on the Parthenon —Phidias, sculptor and general director; and Ictinus and Callicrates, architects. Their greatest achievement, perhaps the greatest architectural work of antiquity, was this temple to Athena. In appearance it is a columned rectangle in Doric style. In reality it is an extraordinary series of refinements that, taken together, produce optical harmony: horizontal lines curve in the middle; the columns bulge in the center, taper at the top and lean slightly inward; flutings diminish in width as they rise. Iron in the marble gives the structure a golden glow. Plutarch, who first saw the Acropolis' buildings when they were 500 years old, claimed they must have been "venerable as soon as they were built."

CEREMONIAL RIDER *of the Panathenaic procession wears his best clothes to make a splendid show. He is wearing a Thracian riding hat with ear coverings, while his cloak and tunic are Athenian.*

THE HISTORIC PARTHENON, *although a ruin, still clearly shows what its builders hoped to achieve more than 2,400 years ago. For nearly 900*

years it was a temple to Athena, for nearly 1,000 years a Christian church, for 200 years a Moslem mosque. Then, in 1687, the Venetian forces besieging the Turks on the Acropolis dropped a shell that exploded a powder magazine, thus destroying the inside of the Parthenon.

THE TEMPLED GODDESS
ADORED BY ATHENS

Religious ceremonies and public worship were held at altars outside the temples; the interiors were for private prayers. Here in a majestic half light one might come face to face with an awesome divinity. Changing shadows could impart human expressions to the statue. Today no man knows exactly what the interior of the Parthenon looked like. The model shown here was constructed especially for this book on the basis of the best modern scholarship. It remains, however, an informed guess. There were two rooms inside. In one stood the statue of Athena the Virgin, made by Phidias in gold and ivory around a wooden core. In a second room, there were other treasures of the temple: the Persian Xerxes' silver-footed throne, for instance, on which he had sat and watched his forces defeated by the Athenian fleet at Salamis. But nothing was more important than the statue. Thus when Pericles' foes wished to strike at him through his friend Phidias, they accused the artist of stealing some of the gold given to him to make the statue. Since the gold plates were removable Phidias was able to take them down, weigh them and prove that all the gold was still there. But their enemies were not satisfied. They next accused Phidias of sacrilege in carving pictures of himself and of Pericles on Athena's shield. Pericles stood by him to the end. Fortunately most of his great works had been completed when the attack came. Pericles continued in his post as a general for a few more years until his death.

ON A RAINY DAY *the pillars and walls of the south side of the Parthenon stand desolate. The north and south walls were blank. The temple received its light from doors facing east and west.*

THE GODDESS ATHENA *is shown in this reconstruction clad in sumptuous robes. In her right hand is a statue of Nike, or Victory. On her helmet was a Sphinx and on her breast an ivory Medusa.*

6

GREEK AGAINST GREEK

Along with its incredible display of energy in matters relating to the mind and spirit, Periclean Athens was also busily engaged in expanding its trade and political influence. It had firmly established itself as a sea power; now it began to cast covetous eyes on its neighbors on the mainland. The Greek states, which had hitherto maintained a precarious balance of power among themselves, were now drawn into one of two camps—Athens' or Sparta's—and soon war became inevitable. The Peloponnesian War began in 431 B.C. and lasted, with one brief interval of peace, until 404 B.C. It was a long war, bitter and demoralizing, and it ended for Athens in disaster. And yet all through it, and even after its end, Athens continued to be the wellspring of Greek intellectual and artistic life, producing playwrights and philosophers whose contributions were different in spirit from those of the age of Pericles, but every bit as extraordinary.

At the outbreak of the war in 431 B.C., Greece was divided in two. The Spartan Alliance took in most of the Peloponnesus, the Isthmus of Corinth, and Megara. The Athenian Empire embraced the islands of the Aegean and the coast of Asia Minor. Sparta was conservative, aristocratic, resolute in its determination to maintain the existing state of affairs. Athens was aggressively democratic, even revolutionary, and determined to spread its gospel to new places. The war was therefore an important one in principle. It also became an important one to history, largely through the effort of one man, the historian Thucydides, who wrote a superb account of it in his book *The Peloponnesian War*. Thucydides himself participated in the war, and all through it took notes on it. Afterward he collected eyewitness accounts of its events, and examined documents and battle sites. He set down his findings with scientific care and detachment, but his book, at the same time, is full of revealing details about personalities and intelligent interpretations of the issues over which each engagement was fought.

Although the war's underlying cause was Sparta's deep distrust of Athens, the incidents which led up to its outbreak were, as so often happens, quite trivial. One of Sparta's leading allies was Corinth, a commercial and colonial power whose

MARCHING TO WAR, *a soldier on a Sixth Century B.C. wine-and-water mixing bowl found at Vix, France, is protected by a knee-to-neck round shield, bronze greaves around his legs and a helmet equipped with cheek guards.*

WAR OF THE BROTHERS

THE GREAT CAMPAIGNS *of the Peloponnesian War are shown on the map. Many unconventional tactics were employed. Besieging Plataea, the Spartans tried to build a mound from which their archers could shoot over the walls. The Plataeans tunneled to the mound and removed the dirt from the bottom as fast as the Spartans put it on top. When the Spartans brought up battering rams the Plataeans lassoed them and pulled them inside the walls. At sea the Spartans drew up 47 ships in a circle, prows outward. Twenty Athenian ships sailed around and around them, forcing them into an ever smaller circle until the Spartan ships were all entangled and easy prey. At Delium the Boeotians, Sparta's allies, used a cauldron of burning coals, a hollowed-out tree and a bellows to make a flamethrower that destroyed the defensive walls.*

ALLIANCES IN 431 B.C.

- ATHENIAN EMPIRE AND ALLIES
- SPARTAN CONFEDERACY
- NEUTRAL STATES
- ATHENIAN VICTORY
- ATHENIAN DEFEAT

interests were sharply competitive with Athens'. In 433 B.C., Athens formed an alliance with the colony of Corcyra, which had been founded by Corinth but was temporarily at odds with it. At almost the same time Athens also interfered in the affairs of another Corinthian settlement at Potidaea. Corinth objected and warned Athens to stop. Pericles, feeling that war was imminent, retaliated by imposing a total embargo on trade with Megara, a state that bordered on Attica but belonged to the Spartan Alliance. He regarded Megara, situated on the strategic Corinthian Isthmus, as a serious threat to the Athenian Empire. With this series of events, and at Corinth's urging, Sparta declared war on Athens, and Pericles accepted the challenge.

Pericles had two great assets, the Athenian fleet and the Athenian treasury, and one great liability —the Athenian army was no match for the Spartans. Consequently he proposed to let the enemy invade Attica, calculating that the city of Athens could hold out behind its fortifications. Meanwhile he would use the Athenian fleet to inflict damage wherever it could. The whole plan was based on the assumption that Sparta would eventually be worn out.

Despite Pericles' prestige, his plan became unpopular. Athens itself was secure behind its walls and, with its access to the sea, was assured of a supply line for food. But the surrounding countryside was annually devastated by Spartan invaders who destroyed the grain, the orchards, and in particular the olive trees, which take many years to become productive and were the main wealth of Athenian citizens. For safety the villagers were brought into Athens, which soon became hideously overcrowded, and in 430 B.C. the city fell easy prey to an appalling pestilence, possibly typhus.

At this point Pericles was bitterly attacked for the war's lack of progress. Perhaps in response, he led an expedition by sea against Epidaurus, on the Peloponnesus, besieging the city but failing to capture it. Then he went on to lay waste several other cities farther along the Peloponnesian coast. When he arrived home he found Attica devastated by a 40-day Spartan siege, and Athens shaken in spirit and anxious for peace. The Athenians, blaming him for their misfortunes, voted him out of office,

and tried and fined him for misuse of public funds. Not long afterward, however, they re-elected him, realizing that, whatever his failings, he was the best leader they had. One year later Pericles died. His death, by plague, is described by Plutarch as being "a dull and lingering distemper, attended with various changes and alterations, leisurely, by little and little, wasting the strength of his body, and undermining the noble faculties of his soul." For Athens, the loss was tragic.

The men who succeeded Pericles as leaders of the Assembly rivaled him neither in authority nor judgment. One faction, led by the rich and respectable Nicias, wanted to sue Sparta for peace; the other, under the violent demagogue Cleon, wanted to continue fighting. Nicias was an honest but timid man who was sometimes accused of using his wealth to buy the Athenians' favor. He sponsored, says Plutarch, "dramatic exhibitions, gymnastic games, and other public shows, more sumptuous and more splendid than had ever been known in his or in former ages." Cleon was the son of a tanner and had risen to power during the war through a combination of shrewdness, daring and eloquence. He

called himself "the people's watchdog," but not all Athenians agreed with his own evaluation of himself. Thucydides suggests that he opposed peace because "he thought that in a time of peace and quiet people would be more likely to notice his evil doings and less likely to believe his slander of others."

Between them, Nicias and Cleon kept Athens and the Athenian cause in a constant state of turmoil, disagreeing over policy and exposing their disagreements in angry debates. On at least one occasion the Assembly reversed itself within the space of two days. In 428 B.C., Mytilene, on the island of Lesbos, tried unsuccessfully to bolt the Athenian Empire. To punish the city for this act of disloyalty Cleon persuaded the Assembly to vote death for its whole adult male population. A ship was sent to the Athenian fleet with orders to carry this out, but the next day, over Cleon's angry protests, the Assembly countermanded the order and sent a second ship, which, by exerting a prodigious effort, arrived ahead of the first one.

On another occasion Nicias called Cleon's bluff in the handling of the blockade of the island of

Sphacteria, offshore from the Spartan seaport of Pylos. Athenian forces had occupied Pylos in 425 B.C. but a contingent of Spartans still held Sphacteria. The siege had dragged on for many months when Cleon, in the Assembly, contemptuously announced that if he had been in command of the Athenian forces, he could have taken the island handily. Piqued, Nicias turned the command over to him, and demanded that he make good on his claim. Cleon tried to renege, but could not, so he sailed off, with a parting promise to accomplish his task within 20 days. To everyone's surprise, he did. The Spartans on Sphacteria surrendered, an almost unprecedented event in Greek history.

To many Athenians it seemed a good time to stop the war altogether—while Athens was ahead and could exact favorable terms. But Cleon, inflated by his success, insisted on continuing the struggle. Almost immediately, Athens began to lose ground. It was defeated first at Delium in Boeotia in 424 B.C., and then at Amphipolis in Thrace in 422 B.C. Cleon himself was killed in the battle at Amphipolis, and so was the Spartan general, Brasidas, a man so personable that even his enemies admired him. Thucydides says that the recollection of his gallantry and wisdom was the chief factor in creating pro-Spartan feeling among the Athenian allies later in the war.

In 421 B.C. a peace treaty was signed, but the peace had little chance of being kept. Sparta's allies felt that they had been defrauded of legitimate gains, while at Athens a younger, more confident generation made bold plans. They were led by a figure new to Athenian politics, the young Alcibiades, a kinsman of Pericles. Alcibiades had been brought up in Pericles' household, but he was a very different sort of man. Unusually gifted in looks, intelligence and wealth, he was also ambitious, insolent and extravagant. As long as his personal ambitions coincided with Athens' gain, he was accounted a

vigorous patriot and was loved and admired. But he was also feared.

A spirit of recklessness, of which Alcibiades was an extreme representative, now pervaded Athens. Added to it was a new ruthlessness. In the words of Thucydides, "War is a stern teacher; in depriving them of the power of easily satisfying their daily wants, it brings most people's minds down to the level of their actual circumstances." Neither Athens nor Sparta any longer allowed considerations of decency and honor to stand in the way of possible advantage. In 427 B.C., when the Spartans captured the city of Plataea, an Athenian ally, they put to death all the people who surrendered. In the winter of 416-415 B.C., when the island of Melos refused to join the Athenian Empire, Athens killed all men of military age and enslaved the rest of the inhabitants.

But not everyone was callous about such acts. In 415 B.C., Euripides produced his *Trojan Women*, dramatizing the injustices and horrors of war. In it, Hecuba, the captured Trojan queen, says:

> Who am I that I sit
> Here at a Greek king's door,
> Yea, in the dust of it?
> A slave that men drive before,
> A woman that hath no home,
> Weeping alone for her dead;
> A low and bruised head,
> And the glory struck therefrom.

In 419 B.C. Alcibiades undertook a new offensive against Sparta on the pretext that Sparta had not carried out the obligations of the peace treaty. The climax of this campaign came a year later, when, despite careful preparations, the Athenians and their allies were soundly defeated by the Spartans at Mantinea. But the collapse of this venture did not wholly discredit Alcibiades. He continued to control a powerful, if extreme, element of public opinion, and soon had devised other, more ingenious plans. If Sparta could not be defeated by frontal attack, he would destroy it by other means. He proposed to leave Sparta alone for the time being and strengthen Athens by incorporating the Greek colonies in the west, notably in Sicily, into the Empire. If this could be done, Corinthian trade, the financial backbone of the Spartan Alliance, would be mortally stricken and Sicily's rich yield of crops and cattle would fall to Athens. In addition Sicilian manpower would provide a new source of troops for military service. But even more glittering prizes may have bewitched the Athenian imagination— across the narrow strait from Sicily was the rich Phoenician city of Carthage, which controlled the whole trade of the western Mediterranean.

The immediate objective of the Sicilian campaign was the city of Syracuse and, on the pretext of protecting neighboring Sicilian cities from Syracusan tyranny, a large-scale expedition was launched. It sailed from Piraeus, carrying the vast hopes and exalted ambitions of an admiring crowd of well-wishers. Thucydides says that "almost the entire population of Athens, citizens and foreigners, went down to Piraeus . . . full of hope and full of lamentation at the same time, thinking of the conquests that might be made and thinking, too, of those whom they might never see again."

The Syracusan expedition was one of those historical events which seem in retrospect to have been doomed to disaster. No effort was spared to make it a success, and every effort failed. It was led by two of the most important men in Athens, Nicias and Alcibiades, and one of the best Athenian generals, Lamachus. Actually, Nicias had opposed the project in the Assembly and in one sense was a drawback to the expedition—he had no gift for daring enterprise. Alcibiades could have supplied the imagination and initiative which Nicias lacked but,

upon reaching Sicily, he was ordered home to stand trial for a gross act of sacrilege against images of the god Hermes. Knowing what awaited him at Athens, Alcibiades instead defected to Sparta and, lightly changing his allegiance, gave advice to the Spartans which was to do severe harm to Athens.

After a slow start, the Athenians succeeded in blockading Syracuse by sea, and seemed on the point of cutting it off by land as well. But then two events spoiled their chances. Lamachus was killed and the hopes of Syracuse were revived by the arrival of a Spartan general, Gylippus, sent on the advice of Alcibiades. Nicias was deeply discouraged. Toward the end of 414 B.C. he sent a message to Athens: "The time . . . has come for you to decide either to recall us, or else to send out another force, both naval and military, as big as the first, with large sums of money, and also someone to relieve me of the command, as a disease of the kidneys has made me unfit for service."

In the year 413 B.C., the situation grew even more menacing. The Athenian army, unable either to surround Syracuse or breach its defenses, was encamped in a low-lying, marshy area. The troops contracted fever, and Nicias' illness worsened. When the requested reinforcements finally arrived, led by Demosthenes, they were too late; they sailed into the harbor only to find themselves in danger of being trapped. They should have withdrawn as swiftly as possible, but Nicias delayed because the moon was in eclipse and he was superstitious about moving at such a time. Thucydides remarks that he "was rather over-inclined to divination and such things."

By the time Nicias did give the order to move, the Athenian cause was hopeless. The Greek ships were unable to break out of the harbor, and the army, trying to retreat southward by land, was too disorganized and demoralized to fend off the Syracusans. Nicias and Demosthenes surrendered and

were put to death. A fortunate few of their troops became house slaves, but the rest were put into Sicilian stone quarries, where, according to Thucydides, "they were crowded together in a narrow pit, where . . . they suffered first from the heat of the sun and the closeness of the air; and then, in contrast, came on the cold autumnal nights, and the change in temperature brought disease among them. Lack of space made it necessary for them to do everything on the same spot; and besides there were the bodies all heaped together on top of one another . . . so that the smell was insupportable . . . their sufferings were on an enormous scale; their losses were, as they say, total; army, navy, everything was destroyed, and, out of many, only few returned."

Yet such was the resilience of the Athenian spirit, and the strength of its naval power, that it continued to fight for another 10 years. New ships were built, new crews trained, and the routes to the Black Sea and its vital grain ports were kept open. At the same time Athens was sufficiently self-critical to wonder if something might be wrong with its democratic system of government, and for a short time it experimented with more traditional forms. From June to September, 411 B.C., for instance, it placed the entire administration, including control of money matters, in the hands of an appointed Council of 400 men, 40 from each of the 10 Attic tribes. Other experiments followed, but none of them inspired confidence, and eventually full democracy was restored. At one point, for almost a year, the traitorous Alcibiades, no longer

welcome in Sparta, was actually allowed to return and serve as general, but he failed to fulfill the city's hopes for strong and effective leadership, and was not re-elected.

Despite these vacillations, Athens might have continued the war but for three setbacks. One was the defection of many of the Athenian allies, including Chios, Miletus, Mytilene, Rhodes and Abydos, to the Spartan side in 412-411 B.C. The second was Sparta's decision, in defiance of its own principles and Greek tradition, to form an alliance with Persia; among other advantages, this move supplied Sparta with ample funds. The third calamity for Athens was Sparta's decision to build a fleet and oppose Athens at sea.

The end, when it came, was sudden. The Athenian fleet, waiting in the harbor of Aegospotami, in Thrace, was caught off guard and destroyed by the Spartan fleet, under Lysander, while the Athenian crews were ashore eating a meal. The news reached Athens on a day in late summer, 405 B.C., and "on that night no man slept." Faced by starvation and stymied by fruitless negotiations, Athens surrendered to Lysander in April 404 B.C. By the terms of peace it lost all its foreign possessions, forfeited its fleet, agreed to pull down the walls of Piraeus and the Long Walls between Piraeus and Athens, and pledged itself to become an ally of Sparta.

For Athens the war had been a total war. The lands had been invaded and devastated, and the fighting had reached the very walls of the city. Men of mature years had been called up for active service; communication other than by sea had been

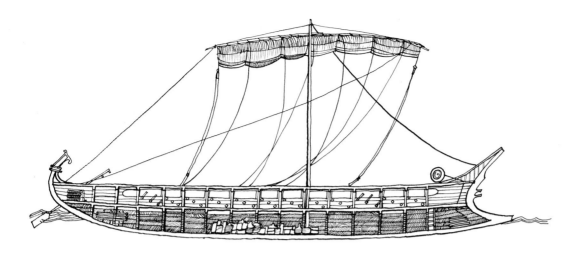

scanty and perilous; food, never abundant, had often been scarce.

Yet despite the huge drain on its physical resources, the city never abandoned its interest in the arts. During the worst phases of the war Athens raised two of the loveliest temples on the Acropolis, the little temple to Athena Nike and the Erechtheum. In the very midst of the plague Sophocles wrote his masterpiece, *Oedipus Rex*, and in the closing days of the war he comforted the Athenian people with the message of his last play, *Oedipus at Colonus*. Oedipus in this play is old and has suffered long for his misdeeds, but is finally permitted to die in peace. Sophocles gave him some memorable and reassuring lines:

> *For every nation that lives peaceably, there*
> *will be many others to grow hard and push*
> *their arrogance to extremes: the gods attend*
> *to these things slowly. But they attend to*
> *those who put off God and turn to madness!*

Fifteen of the 19 surviving plays of Euripides were written during the war, including *Heracles* and *Electra*, both of which are deeply compassionate and understanding—inspired, no doubt, by the experience of Athens.

During the war Aristophanes continued to produce his ebullient comedies. In *Acharnians* he made fun of the war party and in *Birds* he ridiculed the heady fancies current at the time of the invasion of Syracuse. Despite his irreverence Aristophanes loved his city and often gave it wise ad-

vice. In the end he even gave it comfort. *Frogs*, an enchanting spoof of poetry, was written to soften the blow of defeat when defeat seemed imminent.

In one sense the war enriched the Athenian spirit by forcing it to look deeply into many matters and infusing it with courage and nobility. In another sense it degraded it. During the long years of strife something sinister and corrupt crept into Athenian life. Partly it was the product of physical hardship, but it was much more the product of the spiritual erosion that inevitably accompanies a prolonged war. Pericles had been proud of Athens' free spirit of inquiry, but the Athens of Alcibiades' day cared more about authority than freedom. Alcibiades himself termed democracy "an acknowledged folly," and Athens, although it eventually threw him out, tended to agree with him. For the old religion and morality, it substituted a belief in "might makes right" and twisted the old concept of personal honor into personal advancement.

Lacking a sense of honor, people no longer behaved honorably but masked their behavior with fine words. The old love of serious argument was debased into ingenious dispute, by which the most despicable actions were made to appear excellent. The old admiration for intellectual prowess degenerated into a respect for a certain kind of craftiness, the ability to advance a cause by whatever means came to mind. The chief exponents of these views happened to be among a group of men called Sophists. A Sophist was simply a traveling teacher and the doctrine he expounded was very much his own, often quite unlike any other Sophist's. Many of them, however, practiced—and preached—a method of argument based on clever, specious reasoning. But they were very much in demand, because they were thought to purvey the latest ideas and to equip their students for success in public life. Thrasymachus, for instance, who taught that rule by force was a law of nature, had a considerable vogue among the young men around Alcibiades.

Not all Sophists, however adroit their arguments, were concerned only with matters of worldly success. Some of them were entirely serious, true descendants of an older generation of scientists and philosophers whose goal had been knowledge. Protagoras, pondering the nature of the gods, carried his speculations further than any previous Greek by concluding: "I cannot know that they exist, nor yet that they do not exist." For this "impiety" Protagoras was forced to flee Athens. Men were afraid of such radical notions; they may even have imagined them to be downright harmful while the war dragged on and Athens needed whatever moral strength it could muster.

It was Socrates, another Sophist accused of "impiety," who inspired the flowering of a new philosophy in Athens. But that was not to happen until a generation later. Athens had first to recover from the immediate effects of the war, which left it economically exhausted and torn by political problems.

Athens' political difficulties stemmed in large part from Sparta's bungling attempts to install a government favorable to Spartan ideas. Sparta gave its support to the conservative, antidemocratic element in Athenian politics, and appointed a ruling council of 30 men who were afterward referred to in Athenian history as the Thirty Tyrants. Instead of governing, the Thirty spent their time persecuting their old opponents, the democrats. They confiscated property and condemned an appalling number of men to death, with little regard for law and order. In less than a year the people of Athens rose, deposed the Thirty and drove them from the city.

Elsewhere Sparta's policies were equally inept. The victory had given it an unparalleled opportunity to unite, at long last, the Greek city-states. But Spartan misrule soon had Greece more divided than ever. Its kings, accustomed to absolute authority at home, did not know how to treat men used to being their own masters. Its generals, trained only for war, were quickly corrupted by the prospects of gain in their new positions as garrison commanders. Its local governments were brutal and bloodthirsty and incompetent. Sparta's gains were quickly spent. In 371 B.C. it was decisively removed from power by the defeat of its army at the Battle of Leuctra by a Theban army under a gifted general named Epaminondas.

At Athens, with the departure of the Thirty Tyrants, a measure of democracy was restored and the city began to mend its shattered economic life. The expenses of the war had emptied its treasury and it could no longer, as in former times, draw upon the treasury of the Delian League. Athenian markets in the Mediterranean had been encroached upon by traders from other countries not involved in the war. In the port cities of Sicily and Italy, for example, Athenian ships now had to share their commerce with ships from Carthage. But Athens' trade in the Black Sea area was still intact, and it now began to concentrate its shipping there, calling on ports as distant as the Crimea. By 370 B.C. Athens was sufficiently prosperous to attempt a restoration of its Empire. At best the attempt was successful only in part and by 360 B.C. had clearly failed, but the city had obviously recovered enough vitality to become again the spiritual center of Greece, the "school of Hellas." In this new phase the Athens of Pericles' day was replaced by an Athens that took its attitudes from the ideas of Socrates.

THE DISCUS THROWER *holds the plate-shaped weight palm outward. At first a discus was any object used for throwing. Then a flat disk was used. Stone disks weighed about 15, metal ones 3 to 9 pounds.*

THE PANHELLENIC GAMES

Scarcely a city failed to stage games in honor of the gods, but the attention of all Greece was attracted by the four great Panhellenic festivals: the Olympic Games at Olympia and the Pythian Games at Delphi, both held every four years; and the Nemean Games in Argolis and the Isthmian Games at Corinth, each held every two years. These drew athletes from all parts of Greece. They competed as individuals, not as teams (though their cities gloried in their victories), on a fervently amateur basis. Wars were put aside for the Games; Sparta was fined for violating the sacred truce of the Olympic Games during the Peloponnesian War.

IN A PRE-GAME CEREMONY *a pig is formally slaughtered as a sacrifice. Then the athletes swore they had trained hard for 10 months.*

THE OLYMPIC GLADE

Greatest of the Panhellenic Games were the Olympics, held at Olympia, where the mute ruins of the Palaestra, or training area, stand. Olympia was not a town but a grouping of temples and arenas in the fields. People came to it from all parts of Greece and since there were no permanent houses, they set up tents and slept in the open. Among them were leaders from all the cities who talked high politics; often peace treaties or alliances were arranged at the Games. Also present were horse dealers and shouting vendors of wineskins and food, amulets and votive offerings, for this was not only a religious occasion but also a fair. The crowds flowed to the stadium to see running and jumping events, discus and javelin throwing. They went to the hippodrome, or race course, for the horseback and chariot races. An open space in front of the altar of Zeus was the arena for boxing and wrestling. Elsewhere in the forest of altars and statues could be found artists and poets come to entertain or sell their wares, and at night, there was feasting.

AT THE TRAINING AREA *of Olympia, wind-stirred flowers evoke the*

ghosts of multitudes of people. Here the judges gathered to watch the athletes go through their final preparation before participating in the actual games.

THE CHARIOTEER *was one of the few clothed athletes. Because the victor's crown went not to the driver but to the owner of the chariot and horses, rich men avid for honors sometimes entered as many as seven chariots in the same race.*

THE STARTING SLAB *at Olympia (below), divided to give each runner four feet of lateral room, accommodated 20 men. The racers, who wore no shoes, lined up by positioning their feet according to the grooves that are cut into the stone slab.*

A FIELD OF RUNNERS *is portrayed (right) in an unnatural running position: moving right arms and legs together. Although the artist certainly knew better, he may have wanted to clear away a clutter of arms that was crowding his picture.*

128

RUNNERS AND CHARIOT RACING

Racing—foot racing from such starting blocks as the one at the far left and chariot racing behind such steeds as those above—was the essence of the Games. The opening spectacle of the Olympics was a four-horse chariot race. As many as 40 chariots lined up in the stalls of a triangular, prow-shaped starting gate with its apex facing down the course. The ropes freeing the contestants to run dropped at various intervals calculated to bring all the chariots into a line at the start of the race. The distance was nearly nine miles, or 12 double laps back and forth between two posts in the ground. Since swinging four galloping horses around a stone post sent the chariots skidding wildly, the races were run off in a dust storm of collisions, spills and upendings. Very few starters managed to finish the course.

IN WAR GEAR *citizen warriors compete in a special race that many Greek spectators apparently considered comic. But the event was, nonetheless, very popular and 25 shields were on hand at Olympia for the use of the contestants.*

A FIERCE COMPETITIVE SPIRIT

Competition at Olympia was fierce. Jockeys rode all out without saddle or stirrups. Jumpers carried weights in their hands which they swung to gain forward impetus. The *pankration* was a combination boxing and wrestling, kicking and strangling fight to the finish with nothing barred save gouging and biting. Breaking an opponent's fingers was also condemned. Save in rare instances the games were contested in the nude. To the Greeks nudity seemed the natural way to exercise—and it fostered pride in physical fitness and shame at being flabby.

A BOXING TRIUMPH *comes when the victor gets in a crack to the head and the loser, left, raises a finger to acknowledge defeat.*

EVENTS OF THE PENTATHLON, *depicted on the cup at the left, were designed to choose all-round athletes who could do well in a series of five contests, rather than specialists in one sport. Among the pentathletes shown here stands a trainer holding a baton in his hand.*

IN AN ANCIENT BALL GAME, *each side tries to force the other back over its own goal line. A favorite sport of youths in their late teens,* *it had aspects of modern rugby. But this sport was recreation for the Greeks and was not one of their more serious games.*

PASTIMES AND AMUSEMENTS

Training was grinding work. It is not happenstance that the Greek word for public games became the English word "agony." But there were periods of relief from the endless practice. Men might use an idle moment at the training school betting on cat and dog fights like the one at the right, or they could get up a vigorous ball game *(above).* Greek art pictures no end of games whose exact nature must now be guessed at, for there is no other evidence about them than a picture of two men with crooked sticks in what looks like a hockey face-off, or a picture of a man on another's shoulders trying to catch a ball. These were pastimes that never made the Olympics, where there were no team contests—perhaps because the Greek temperament was too hotly competitive for the cooperation required.

ANIMAL FIGHTS, *such as the one being promoted in the picture above, provided amusement and an occasion for gambling in gymnasiums.*

133

THE WINNERS' AWARDS

Winners at the great Panhellenic Games received only garlands—wild olive leaves at the Olympics, pine needles at the Isthmian Games at Corinth, laurel at the Pythian Games at Delphi, and parsley at the Nemean Games in Argolis. Lesser festivals gave valuable prizes: 100 vases of olive oil to the chariot race winner at Athens, cloaks at Pellene, shields at Argos. But there were other benefits as well. In their home cities statues were erected to victors. At times the hero was welcomed through a special hole knocked in the city's walls. He was paraded in triumph through the streets, and poems in his praise were sung in public places. An especially enthusiastic city might give him front-row seats to all public spectacles, make him exempt from taxation and give him free meals. And in Athens, and elsewhere, too, he was given a good round sum in cash.

THE VICTOR'S GARLAND of laurel, awarded winners at Delphi's Games, is re-created over a similar stone wreath now in the theater of Dionysus in Athens. Laurel was sacred to Apollo.

THE VICTOR'S PRIZE at Athens' games was olive oil, in amphorae such as this one. The vase has a picture of Athena on one side and a picture of the game it was given for on the other.

134

A YOUTHFUL WINNER *of the games is shown in this bronze wearing a fillet, or band, around his head. This band will serve to support the garland.*

7
A NEW TIME
OF BRILLIANCE

After 404 B.C., Athens never regained the glory of the Periclean Age because much of that glory arose from beliefs that were now, if not dead, at least eroded. To Athenians a life spent in the service of their city-state had once seemed ideal, but the defeat by Sparta had tarnished that ideal. For a time, during the period when the Sophists held sway over Athenian intellectual life, some men aspired to nothing except getting ahead in the world. Then the ideas of Socrates took hold and gave Athens a new spiritual concern. In the Socratic view, a man's conscience was a better guide to right conduct than the demands of society. An Athens with this belief could not hope to return to the golden days of Pericles, but its accomplishments in the century that followed the war, if less glorious, are no less astonishing. In Plato and Aristotle it produced two of the most extraordinary thinkers who ever lived— the Platonic and Aristotelian systems of thought underlie much of Western philosophy. Fourth Century Athens also raised oratory to a fine art; public speakers gave their discourses the brilliance and style that an earlier age had lavished on drama and poetry.

Socrates was the first exponent in Greece of a morality based on the demands of individual conscience rather than the demands of the state. His teaching took the form of relentless questioning. The Socratic method was based on pitiless examination and skepticism, a combination that may have doomed his search for truth to failure. If nothing can be accepted as true, how can truth be found? And yet the seriousness of Socrates' intentions is beyond question. He was totally opposed to the theories of power and expediency current at the time; he had no personal ambition, refused to take money for his teaching, and tried to order his own life along the simplest of lines. In his own way he was deeply religious, and although he said very little about his beliefs, they played a large part in his life.

Socrates' ruthless inquisitions of traditional Athenian attitudes may have helped to undermine the city's old self-assurance. One segment of the Athenian public thought this to be so, and felt that his teachings were dangerous. In 399 B.C. he was officially accused of introducing strange gods and

MOST LOVELY OF WOMEN *to generations is a statue of Aphrodite, known as the "Venus de Milo" because it was found at Melos. After the Peloponnesian War, though some arts declined, sculpture flourished for over 300 years.*

corrupting the young, and brought to trial. Socrates might have saved himself by recanting, or conceding that he had been at fault, but he refused. On the contrary, he antagonized his judges by defending his actions in a speech which they regarded as arrogant:

Athenians, I am not going to argue for my own sake . . . but for yours, that you may not sin against the God by condemning me, who am his gift to you. For if you kill me you will not easily find a successor to me, who, if I may use such a ludicrous figure of speech, am a sort of gadfly, given to the state by God; and the state is a great and noble steed who is tardy in his motions owing to his very size, and requires to be stirred into life. I am that gadfly which God has attached to the state, and all day long and in all places am always fastening upon you, arousing and persuading and reproaching you. You will not easily find another like me, and therefore I would advise you to spare me.

Athens, condemning him to death, ordered him to drink hemlock. As the poison was taking effect Socrates sat and talked quietly with a group of his friends. The talk was recorded by his pupil Plato, who hailed Socrates as "the wisest and most just and best man" who ever lived, a saint and a martyr. Plato set down all he could remember of Socrates' teaching (Socrates himself never wrote a thing), and his own long and productive life was shaped by Socrates' passion for truth, his uncompromising morality and his belief that "a life without inquiry is not worth living."

When Socrates died, Plato was 30 and seemed destined for a career in public life. He was born into the Athenian aristocracy and was thoroughly schooled in music, mathematics and letters. The

THE SPARTAN WARRIOR, *shown in his cloak and helmet, dominated Greece after the defeat of Athens. Disciplined by life in a harsh military community, the Spartan was the best infantryman of his time. But rigid rule brought its own weaknesses. The warrior caste gradually dwindled; the city refused to enlist new blood and Sparta shrank from strength to insignificance.*

death of his teacher scarred his spirit and altered the course of his life. For a time he left Athens to travel abroad. When he returned to his native city about 385 B.C., he founded a school in the garden called Academus (the school became known as the Academy), where he taught until his death in 347.

Along with many intellectuals of his day Plato was much interested in the science of mathematics, especially geometry. He believed that it was basic to any system of thought, and he liked to call himself a mathematician. In fact, he was a great deal more than this, so much more that it is hard to assign him a label. Plato took his mathematical ideas from the writings of the Pythagoreans, followers of the Sixth Century philosopher who had formulated the Pythagorean theorem every schoolboy knows. Pythagoras' investigations had been concerned with mathematical systems and the mystical meanings of numbers. He had come to believe that the entire universe was constructed upon numerical relationships. It was these abstruse ideas that Plato borrowed and incorporated into his own philosophical system.

Plato set down his philosophy in written dialogues, in each of which a group of people discusses some matter of far-reaching importance. The discussion is always natural and conversational in tone, but in fact it follows a skillfully concealed plan. Socrates is often the leading character, behaving much as he behaved in life. He subjects ideas to keen analysis, reveals cracks and flaws in the reasoning of his colleagues, and reduces his opponents to impotence—but always, and only, for the purpose of discovering the truth. In one dialogue, for instance, Plato has Socrates question a character named Laches on the nature of courage:

Socrates: I am sure, Laches, that you would consider courage to be a very noble quality.

Laches: Most noble, certainly.
Socrates: And you would say that a wise endurance is also good and noble?
Laches: Very noble.
Socrates: But what would you say of a foolish endurance? Is not that, on the other hand, to be regarded as evil and hurtful?
Laches: True.
Socrates: Take the case of one who endures in war, and is willing to fight, and wisely calculates and knows that others will help him, and that there will be fewer and inferior men against him than there are with him; and suppose that he has also advantages of position; —would you say of such a one . . . that he, or some man in the opposing army who is in the opposite circumstances to these and yet endures and remains at his post, is the braver?
Laches: I should say . . . the latter, Socrates.
Socrates: But, surely, this is a foolish endurance?
Laches: That is true.

The *Dialogues* cannot possibly be actual records of Socrates' conversations, but undoubtedly they are developments of his ideas and methods. And the message of the early *Dialogues* is also undoubtedly Socratic. Later on, when Plato began to express his own ideas, he continued to use the dialogue form and even continued to use Socrates as a spokesman. It is characteristic of him that he should have set down his thoughts in this indirect way, and he did it for a reason. He believed that the truth could only be found by arduous search, and could never be presented as dogma. In their slow and careful exploration of philosophical problems from more than one point of view, the *Dialogues* dramatize this search and show how difficult it is to find the truth. They were also intended to illustrate another search: the self-questioning that goes on within a man when he is troubled by large and fundamental issues. Plato may have used the dialogue form—so human and lively and dramatic—as an outlet for his own inner struggles, turning those struggles into a literary drama in which the chief events are ideas.

The dialogue also allowed Plato to express both his actual philosophy and his philosophical attitude —that is, both a body of ideas and a method of arriving at them. Deeply involved in his search for truth, Plato may have believed that the method was the more important of the two, but the scope and quality of his actual philosophy are an astonishing achievement for one man. During the course of his long life Plato expanded and revised many of his ideas, but right from the start his philosophical doctrine was a consistent, highly organized system of thought.

Plato had no liking for the time in which he lived. Far from wishing to revive Periclean Athens, he aimed at an ideal quite remote from it. The accomplishments of men like Miltiades and Themistocles and Pericles meant nothing to him; they had "filled the city with harbors and dockyards and walls and tributes instead of with righteousness and temperance." Even their political ideas seemed to him false, for he believed not in political liberty, but in order. In his *Republic*, and later, his *Laws*, he set down his notions of what a state ought to be. He believed in government by a wise few, especially trained for the task, an intellectual and moral elite. These "philosopher-kings" would be educated from childhood until the age of 35, by which time they would be fit to govern the state. Plato described this ideal education in detail, and went on to lay down the laws and the administrative structure of his ideal state.

These political notions were based on a philosophy that was at once penetrating and all-embracing. Like other mathematicians of his day Plato believed that all matter, however various it appeared to the eye, was governed by a few basic laws. The multiplicity of things perceived by the senses was merely "appearance"; reality, the "real" world, was a world of Forms, or Ideas. It is the Form, or Idea, of a thing which gives it meaning and substance. This world of Forms must be sought through contemplation, though it may sometimes be known through intuition. In either case it was far more important than the world of the senses on which the Greeks set so high a value. Plato attacked the fine arts. He thought them too removed from the world of Ideas. Although he himself was a consummate artist in words, and responded more than he liked to poetry, he wanted poetry excluded from his ideal state because it represented an imperfect approach to reality.

At the same time that he rejected the senses as a source of truth, Plato believed that there was much that lay beyond the scope of rational argument. He insisted that there was truth in the old stories of rewards and punishments after death for actions done in life, and he made these rewards and punishments the cornerstone of his system of morality. Thus his rational philosophy is fortified by a mystical sense of another world. Plato himself attached these beliefs to monotheism. He did not insist on monotheism in others, but he did believe that the religious life was a necessary foundation to morality and law.

Plato's strength lies in this combination of mysticism and logic. Once his assumptions are granted, everything seems to follow from them. Yet this method of assumption and deduction, so entirely right in mathematics, runs into trouble when it is applied to the physical universe. When Plato set out to show that the physical world, too, must obey certain rules, he dealt a cruel blow to science. To Plato, these rules were God-given. God was the great artificer. Physical phenomena were to be explained, not by looking at them, but by speculating on why God had made them so. Thus Plato ignored

A NEW POWER BORN IN BATTLE

In the mid-Fourth Century B.C., as Macedonia was gaining supremacy in Greece, on the neighboring peninsula of Italy another new power was emerging—Rome. Tales of bloody battles and lofty heroism dominate the legends and early history of the nation which began as a city on the Tiber. According to one legend, the Romans were required by the gods to sacrifice their greatest gift in order to save the Republic. A young soldier, Marcus Curtius, declared that Rome's chief asset was Roman courage. Then, on horseback, he plunged into a deep chasm that had opened up in the Forum. The moment of his sacrifice is depicted in the relief at left.

In a series of local wars the Romans pushed outward from the Tiber. At first Rome imposed treaties of alliance on its vanquished neighbors, becoming the leader and the chief beneficiary of the Latin League. Inevitably this arrangement provoked revolts. But in 338 B.C., the very year that Philip of Macedon confirmed his dominance in Greece, Rome finally defeated and subjugated its former allies. With all local rivals absorbed into its political system, Rome was now free to defend its interests against other enemies. The new wars that followed made Rome master of the whole peninsula by 265 B.C.

the need for observation and experiment which is the basis of science. In rejecting all of Athens' past accomplishments, he even rejected its scientific successes.

In the end Plato's main conclusions seem wrong. His ideal state was not only impossible to realize, as he knew, but was based on postulates that ran counter to human nature. The collapse of Athens had so frightened him that he was prepared to impose a rigid order even on the activities of the mind, and this carried order too far.

Plato's philosophical system and marvelous language make him one of the most gifted men who ever lived. Nothing was beyond the reach of his subtle, discriminating intellect. But he represented the antithesis of almost everything that had made Greece great. He believed that action was less important than thought, that personal success in itself had no value, that political liberty was a fancy name for disorder. He turned men's attention away from the world of the senses and the life of action to a transcendent, invisible, abstract world. This was indeed a revolution.

Plato's work was continued, and often criticized and contradicted, by Aristotle, who came from Stagirus in Macedonia at the age of 17 to study at Plato's Academy. In volume his writings were even greater than Plato's, although not all of them were, strictly speaking, his own. Parts of Aristotle's work were done by assistants working under his guidance, but his personality dominates every piece of writing that bears his name. Even the literary characteristics of these writings are Aristotle's own. Unlike Plato's elegant dialogues, Aristotle's mature writing is shaped into closely reasoned treatises in which concern for style or phrasing is sacrificed to clarity and conciseness of thought.

Aristotle was rightly called by the poet Dante

"the master of them that know." Almost no branch of knowledge seems to have been alien to him. Essentially his approach to all knowledge was that of an experimental scientist. Although he took the whole world of knowledge as his domain, his outlook remained scientific. If Plato was fundamentally a mathematician, Aristotle was fundamentally a biologist. Plato rejected the senses as being untrustworthy; Aristotle accepted them as one of the most important sources of knowledge and as the means for discovering the laws that govern the physical world.

Aristotle enormously advanced the inquiries of the scientists who had preceded him. He examined the biological structure of living things and devised classifications for all kinds of plants and animals. Later he took a similar approach to weather, to metaphysics and logic, to human society and human behavior, and even to the art of words in rhetoric and poetry. In each case he first collected and arranged the evidence; then drew up distinctions and classifications; and finally proceeded to general conclusions that were always balanced, perceptive and well supported by evidence. He believed in both experiment and theory, and his whole work is inspired by a common sense so cool and balanced that it often seems impossible to conceive of an approach other than Aristotle's.

In examining human societies Aristotle did not reject Athens' recent past. Instead, he tried to see what was good and bad in it by analyzing the nature of political constitutions, describing both their strengths and weaknesses. He was profoundly human, a trait not always visible in his scientific writings, but fully exposed in his *Ethics*. This treatise combined Aristotle's own generous conception of the good life with the personal morality introduced by Socrates and the intellectual virtues which Plato had brought to the fore. To Aristotle, the goal of every action was happiness, but not necessarily pleasure. Happiness came from the full use of one's essential nature. In defining this goal he displayed his deepest strength as a philosopher: his tolerance and wisdom, his lack of angry or absurd prejudices. Modern man has inherited his sense of a single universe that encompasses every level of existence, from the behavior of animals to the rules of correct thinking, a universe that rewards inquirers with the conviction that it is ultimately intelligible and both human and divine.

The influence of both Plato and Aristotle has been incalculable. It has been said that some men are born Platonists, and others Aristotelians: that is, in every age some men follow a system of thought in which everything is worked out from abstract principles by stern logic, while other men follow a system in which everything is examined in detail and conclusions are drawn cautiously. Plato has always been a philosopher for mystics, and a political guide for advocates of unity and order. He provided the foundations of a philosophy which, in different forms, infused religious thought for several centuries and eventually passed into Christianity, where it still exerts an influence. By a roundabout route his political ideas passed on to modern authoritarian thinkers, where, in a debased form, they too still exert an influence. Aristotle laid down the principles on which science was pursued for centuries. When

these principles were forgotten in Europe, the Arab world preserved them. In the 13th Century A.D., Arab scholars in North Africa, Sicily and Spain returned them to the West, where they formed the groundwork for the resurgence of science in modern times.

In one way, however, both Plato and Aristotle were failures as theorists. Neither of them saw a way out of the political tangle left in Greece by the Peloponnesian War; neither was interested in the unity of the Greek states; both assumed that the city-state was the only possible center for a civilized, Hellenic life. In the first years of the Fourth Century B.C. one Greek, Dionysius of Syracuse, had built a substantial empire in Sicily and southern Italy, but this feat impressed neither of the philosophers. Dionysius' empire hardly survived the death of its creator, and Plato and Aristotle may have thought it an eccentric and unnatural enterprise which could never be maintained. Yet in the middle of the century the situation began to change, not in Greece proper, but on its northern frontier—in Macedonia.

Macedonia stood in a somewhat ambiguous relation to the Greek world. Its kings, who were of Greek descent, aspired to be Greeks in the fullest sense. But they ruled over a mixed people, and their rule was despotic, not democratic. The Macedoni-

ans had fought against the Greeks in the Persian Wars, and their contribution to Greek civilization had hitherto been trifling. In 359 B.C., Philip II succeeded to the throne of Macedonia, and determined to make himself master of all Greek lands. He began by extending his control into the outlying regions of Macedonia, then he moved south into Thessaly and east into Thrace.

By exploiting the mines of Pangaeum in Thrace, which yielded him 1,000 talents of gold a year (the equivalent of eight million dollars today), Philip amassed enough money to create an army that made him the foremost military commander of his time. It was a professional army, trained to fight in a new phalanx formation—a solid yet flexible body of men moving in close order, sometimes 16 ranks deep, and armed with spears 14 feet long. Philip's skill in diplomacy matched his military talent. He encouraged dissension among the Greek states, and while they fought each other he increased his forces and added to his domains. Sometimes, instead of annexing a state by military force, he tied it to him by alliances in marriage. Philip had, in all, six or seven wives.

By 352 B.C., he had reached Thermopylae, and was preparing to march on Delphi, whose sacred shrine of Apollo made it the center of Greek religious life. Insofar as the Greeks looked anywhere for leadership against this new threat, they looked to Athens. But Athens was divided in its feelings toward Philip. Athenian policy was discussed with much power and eloquence by a new generation of orators, men who brought to speechmaking the same force and skill which an earlier generation had brought to poetry. One side was led by Isocrates, who held that the real danger to Athens was the Persians, still sporadically active across the Aegean. In 346 B.C., Isocrates appealed to Philip to unite the Greeks and take the offensive against Persia. But in the war of words he was outclassed by a master of oratory, Demosthenes, the greatest of all Greek speakers.

Demosthenes had no humor, no lightness of touch, but he had extraordinary oratorical power. Appealing to his countrymen to resist the tyrant who meant to overwhelm them, he mounted a powerful case against Philip, driving each point home with relentless force. Demosthenes may have lacked Pericles' sense of Athens' mission, but he made up for it in the ardor of his love for the city. Athens meant everything to him. He used all his gifts of argument and persuasion to make the Athenians fight for their liberty. In the first of his attacks upon Philip, the "First Philippic," Demosthenes harangues the Athenians:

> *Observe, Athenians, the height to which the fellow's insolence has soared: he leaves you no choice of action or inaction; he blusters and talks big . . . he cannot rest content with what he has conquered; he is always taking in more, everywhere casting his net round us, while we sit idle and do nothing. When, Athenians, will you take the necessary action? What are you waiting for? Until you are compelled, I presume. But what are we to think of what is happening now? For my own part I think that for a free people there can be no greater compulsion than shame for their position.*

Demosthenes' insight into Philip's intentions was accurate, but only up to a point. He could not comprehend Philip's grand plan, but he did foresee his moves, and made carefully considered and practicable proposals to counter them. Through constant and eloquent argument he got his countrymen to oppose Philip and persuaded Thebes to join Athens in the struggle. But in the summer of 338 B.C., Philip routed the allied force at Chaeronea in Boeo-

tia. After this victory Philip called a congress of all the Greek city-states at Corinth and confederated most of them under his military leadership in the League of Corinth.

In the peace treaties that followed this brief war, Philip was harsh to Thebes but generous to Athens. Undoubtedly a good part of that generosity was occasioned by sentiment. A questionable stranger from the semibarbarian fringes of the civilized Greek world, Philip looked upon Athens as the center of Hellenism and profoundly respected its culture. Although there is no question of his capacity for chicanery and bribery, Philip has been badly treated by posterity. It has seen him largely through the eyes of men like Demosthenes, who feared and hated him and used all their powers of eloquence to denounce him. It is impossible not to admire Demosthenes for his patriotism, and impossible not to sympathize with him as the gallant leader of a lost cause, but it is clear that the system he was struggling to perpetuate had outlived its time and was fated to be absorbed in a larger system.

Philip saw, as few others saw, that Greece was ready for political unity. He was confident that he, and he alone, could unify the Greek city-states, and he succeeded in doing so. He had achieved what theretofore had scarcely been thought possible, except as the loosest kind of alliance. Having united Greece, Philip prepared for even further exploits—the conquest of Persia. But just as he was on the verge of attacking the Persian Empire, he was struck down. In 336 B.C., in the midst of a feast celebrating the marriage of a daughter, Philip was murdered. The murderer may have been a Persian agent, or possibly an agent of Philip's first wife, Olympias. In any case, Olympias' son Alexander now succeeded to his father's throne, at the age of 20. As it turned out, Alexander was to outstrip his remarkable father in military skill, in diplomacy and in the range of his ambitions.

THE ORCHESTRA *(or dancing floor) in Greek theaters was the area used by the chorus, which danced and sang. In the center is the base of an altar.*

ENDURING THEATER

Of the hundreds of Greek plays whose titles are still known, only 45 survive in full, but it is clear from this small remnant that Greek drama ranks among the greatest achievements in the whole history of theater. The origins of Hellenic drama are obscure, but it probably began with dances and songs performed in honor of the god Dionysus. Gradually developing from this choral beginning, the Greek theater came to deal with profound subjects. The tragedies examined the nature of evil in an effort to edify the mind by showing how great and heroic spirits behaved in the presence of evil. In the tragedies of the playwrights Aeschylus, Sophocles and Euripides, this art form achieved its most exalted expression, offering a powerful and profound vision of man's inner nature.

LORD OF THE PLAYS

In the beginning Greek theater was more than dramatic story telling; it was a religious rite honoring Dionysus. Youngest of the gods, Dionysus was the lord of the good life and giver of wine. In his first manifestations he was the god of revelry. Among his followers were women, called maenads. Intoxicated with wine, the maenads raced through the woods at night in torchlit orgiastic revels. But as the drama grew in his name and took on its various forms, Dionysus became a more serious figure. Perhaps because goats were sacred to Dionysus, perhaps because goats were prizes for the best plays, the highest form of the plays came to be called tragedy, which in Greek means "goat song."

A PRANCING MAENAD *wears a snake as headdress and carries a staff and leopard cub. The art of acting, many believe, began in ecstatic dancing of Dionysian rites.*

THE INVENTOR OF WINE, *Dionysus (left) flaunts two symbols: his grapevine and drinking cup. Other symbols—the ivy crown, the panther-skin cloak—stress his role as god of wild things.*

AT THE GRAPE PRESS *Dionysian satyrs marked by horses' tails and ears (above) preside over the making of the wine. One brings up more grapes to be pressed beneath the other's dancing feet.*

EPIDAURUS' GREAT THEATER *contains a circular orchestra with a horse-shoe-shaped theatron, or viewing area, surrounding more than half of* *it. The theatron has 34 rows of steeply banked seats in a lower section and 21 rows above that. Opposite the theatron are the ruins of the pro-*

A GLORIOUS SETTING FOR MAJESTIC DRAMA

The theaters were outdoor auditoriums where large audiences sat upon stone benches. Starting time was daybreak. Often the citizens would sit through three tragedies, a satyr play (a grotesque tragicomic play with actors wearing horses' tails and ears) and a comedy. The theater was considered part of a Greek's education, and everyone was encouraged to come. The admission charge would be refunded to playgoers who could not afford it, and they could ask to be reimbursed for the loss of a day's wages. In Athens during drama festivals all business was suspended, the law courts were closed and prisoners were released from jail. Even women, barred from most public events, were welcomed at the theater.

THE SEAT OF HONOR *in Athens' theater was reserved for the high priest of Dionysus. Other priests claimed 50 of the 67 front-row seats. Then came officials, guests of honor and ordinary citizens.*

skenion (a colonnade that eventually became the stage) and the skene (or scene building), which was both dressing hut and stage backdrop.

A MAKER OF COMEDIES, *the playwright Menander is shown in marble inspecting actors' masks. He holds the mask of a youth. On the table are other masks for a young woman and older man.*

EARLY TRICKS OF THE STAGE

Greek theaters were so large that it was hard to communicate moods and feelings to distant spectators. Masks were used that instantly identified the character as old or young, man or woman, happy or sad. Further to create a larger-than-life appearance, the actor was equipped with thick-soled boots and robes with sleeves. There were other devices: masks with calm expressions on one side and angry ones on the other, allowing the actor to change moods with one swift movement of his head; funnel-shaped mouths in the masks that acted as megaphones to project the voice. There was a rolling contrivance that was used to simulate indoor scenes in the outdoor theater. A derrick permitted actors playing gods to arrive on the stage direct from the heavens. It was called *mechane*—machine—in Greek, from which came the Latin *deus ex machina*, or "god from the machine," a phrase still used to mean any artificial or miraculous event introduced into a story to help solve a plot difficulty.

MASKS FOR TRAGEDY *represent King Priam of Troy and a youth. These are terra-cotta copies of masks, probably made of linen and plaster, once used by Greek actors.*

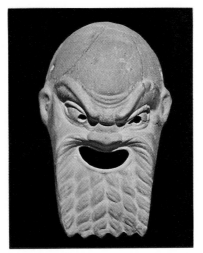

FROZEN EMOTIONS *are etched on the faces of a devilish satyr and a buffoon. Masks helped actors submerge their own personalities in the characters that they played.*

COMEDY, TRAGEDY AND A WREATH OF IVY

Two forms of Greek drama, comedy and tragedy, came to dominate the Dionysian theater, although the other dramatic forms, the dithyramb (or hymn to Dionysus) and satyr play, never died. In Athens two festivals were devoted each year to comedy and tragedy. The City Dionysia festival, in March-April, centered on tragedy. The Lenaea festival, named for the Greek month (January-February) traditionally reserved for celebrating weddings, was devoted chiefly to comedies. The playwrights submitted their work to an official known as the Archon. If the Archon approved he "gave a chorus" to the poet—i.e., assured him that his work would be performed. Competition was fierce and even famous writers were, on occasion, "refused a chorus." The successful dramatist was assigned to a choregus (a rich citizen to pay the costs). The choregus then chose a flute player and a chorus and proceeded with the staging. If the choregus was openhanded, a lavish production emerged. At each festival a jury of citizens judged the plays, and the winners were awarded the Dionysiac wreath of ivy.

IN ROWDY FUN *two tattered drunks (left), wearing grotesque costumes and masks, hold each other up. Marked by an earthy humor, comedies were often trenchant pieces of social criticism.*

IN SOLEMN THOUGHT *Melpomene, Muse of tragedy, contemplates a theatrical mask. This terra-cotta figurine was found at Tanagra, near Athens, which was the center of the best of Greek drama.*

153

THE SPIRIT OF GREEK DRAMA, *representing not a scene from any one play but a mood that expresses them all, is re-created in Athens by its National Theatre group and Greek Army soldiers.*

A FLOURISHING THEATER 2,000 YEARS OLD

With the emergence of Rome as mistress of the West, Greek drama was all but forgotten—save by Roman playwrights. Then, 16 centuries after Christ, some of the plays were printed for the first time. Greek drama began a remarkable recovery. Florentine scholars and artists, trying to re-create Greek tragedy with its choruses, created grand opera. Poets translated or adapted the ancient Greek into rolling French, German and English. Now, there are few countries in the West where Greek drama in some form cannot be seen and heard every year. In America it is regularly presented in Greek on some college campuses. In translation the plays appear in professional theaters in New York and elsewhere, and modern playwrights have experimented with masks and choruses in their own plays. Greek drama has become part of every man's education.

154

"THE TROJAN WOMEN," *Euripides' tragedy of 415 B.C., is shown below in a 1964 New York production. Before the walls of the burning city its women are being given to the victors to serve as their slaves.*

8
ALEXANDER THE GREAT

When Philip of Macedon died in 336 B.C., his son Alexander came into an impressive inheritance. Under Philip's rule Greece was politically much more stable than it had ever been. He had successfully united in the League of Corinth all the city-states except Sparta and he had shrewdly permitted the League's members to retain much of their autonomy. Few of the Greek states had Macedonian garrisons, and no tribute was exacted. Philip had insisted only that the states undertake not to fight among themselves and not to overthrow the government in power at the time the peace treaties were signed. Philip had learned to admire Greece as a young man, when he was a hostage at Thebes. He longed to be a Hellene, to lead the Hellenes, and to make his own people Hellenic.

Even so, the Greeks, to whom individual freedom was the first article of faith, found Philip's control hard to accept. Political stability, however desirable, did not justify the loss of their right to conduct their own affairs. Consequently they could never truly sympathize with the goal of Philip's heir. Alexander dreamed of a whole world that would be confederated—and he came incredibly close to achieving that dream. His near success, ironically, led to the ultimate downfall of the country which was his cultural homeland, just as it had been his father's.

When Alexander ascended the throne at the age of 20, Macedonia's power was so firmly established, and Philip's policy of expansion so well developed, that the young king with his dream of a unified world needed only to pick up where his father had left off. He did so, but in his own way. Though Alexander had his father's ambition and capacity for organization, he had a very different personality. Philip had been a cautious, patient, often devious man; he had never struck without careful planning. The youthful, headstrong Alexander liked to settle problems by immediate action. Making decisions with great speed, he took extraordinary risks; his sheer force and drive overcame the risks.

His favorite book was the *Iliad*. Alexander saw himself as a second Achilles, and not entirely without justice. If ever a man was worthy to be classed with the heroes of Greek legend, Alexander was that man. He was heroic in his physique, his

LEADING THE CHARGE, *Alexander the Great, ardent and brave, fights the Persians. A "monster of celerity," the Macedonian was all over the battlefield cheering his formations forward. In many battles he suffered wounds.*

strength, his courage, in his unflagging endurance and his unconquerable will, in his delight in battle and his confident assumption that he possessed gifts denied to other men. He was no less heroic in the strength of his affections and loyalties, in his unrestrained relaxations, in his generosity to his enemies and his sudden outbursts of furious passion. And although his life and talents were mainly devoted to warfare, he handled the political problems created by his military conquests with brilliant originality.

Aristotle was Alexander's boyhood teacher. The philosopher imbued his young pupil with a love of Greek art and poetry, and instilled in him a lasting interest in philosophy and science. In later life Alexander had philosophers accompany him on campaigns to advise him on political matters. His military retinue also included geographers, botanists, a mineralogist and a meteorologist. Of Aristotle's own particular philosophical bent, Alexander retained almost no trace. It is a paradox that a youthful prince from a semibarbarian state should have conceived of a political system that embraced the whole world, while his wise and sophisticated teacher took the narrow view that the city-state was the ultimate unit of civilization.

Within a year of his accession Alexander extended his dominions northward to the Danube River and westward to the Adriatic Sea. He then turned his attention to Greece, where Thebes and Athens were threatening to bolt the League. Alexander put down the insurrection in Thebes in 335 B.C. Then, to punish the city for what he regarded as treachery, he had its inhabitants slaughtered or sold into slavery and razed all of its buildings except for temples—and the house of Pindar the poet. Pindar himself was dead long since, but Alexander revered him and was eager to prove that even a Macedonian conqueror could be a Hellene. The savage lesson of Thebes brought results. The Athenian

Assembly quickly congratulated Alexander, and the Greek states, with the continuing solitary exception of Sparta, remained Macedonian allies.

Alexander now took on a project that Philip had planned but never carried out: an invasion of Persia. Solid political reasons led him to this decision. For a century Persia had interfered increasingly in Greek affairs and had constantly oppressed the Greek cities in Asia Minor. There was always the dangerous possibility that, under a strong king, it might step up its troublemaking and once again actively take the offensive against Greece. Alexander had personal reasons for the invasion, too. Avid for glory and for identification with Greece, the young King knew no better way to win both than by attacking Greece's ancient foe.

In some ways the invasion was a reckless undertaking. It required a large army to move an enormous distance from its supply bases, through an unfamiliar country, against a power incalculably rich in money and men. Furthermore, Persia was governed by a patriotic and devoted military caste that was eager to show its prowess in war. But the enemy also had weaknesses. The Achaemenid dynasty, which had produced the formidable figures of Darius I and Xerxes, had suffered the usual fate of hereditary despotisms. The current King, Darius III, had come to the throne through the murder of his predecessor. He was no leader—in fact, he was not even a brave man. The best of his generals and satraps might have been able to compensate for his shortcomings, but the rigidly structured hierarchy of the Empire did not give them a chance.

Alexander could also count on help from another quarter. Many of the Empire's subject peoples had no loyalty or affection for their Persian rulers and were unlikely to resist an invading army. In 401-400 B.C. a Greek mercenary army had demonstrated just how easy it was for foreign troops to move across Persia. The mercenaries were in the

FROM A PERSIAN PALACE *comes this relief of a camel being led in tribute to the Emperor. Part of a panel on a stairway in Darius' palace at Persepolis, it depicted for ordinary people who were not allowed to enter the Audience Hall what went on there. Alexander burned the palace, legends say, to satisfy a whim of lovely Thais, who was the mistress of one of his generals, Ptolemy.*

service of Cyrus, a rebellious Persian Prince. Seeking the throne of his brother, Artaxerxes II, Cyrus led his 10,000 Greeks toward Babylon and got as far as the Euphrates River. There he was killed, and the Greeks were left leaderless. A young Athenian, Xenophon, later wrote of their retreat in a famous book, *Anabasis.* Harassed by enemy attacks, plagued by bad weather and hampered by unfamiliar terrain, they made their way back, almost 1,300 miles, to the Black Sea.

The Persians had been unable to destroy the Greek mercenaries of Cyrus. Alexander, with his far stronger army, had good reason to believe that he could win. In 334 B.C. he crossed the Hellespont, which Xerxes had crossed in the opposite direction nearly a century and a half before. Soon afterward he defeated the Persian forces gathered to meet him on the Asian side at the River Granicus. From the spoils of this victory he sent 300 suits of Persian armor back to Athens. With them went the message, "Alexander, the son of Philip, and the Greeks, except the Spartans, have won this spoil from the barbarians of Asia," thus expressing in one brief and self-assured sentence his contempt for the Persians, his even greater contempt for the Spartans, and his conviction that he was furthering a Greek cause.

As the campaign progressed, Alexander's plan expanded. Originally his purpose had been simply to destroy the Persian army. Before long he had decided to take over the whole Persian Empire. And he went on to achieve this aim without losing a single battle. Of all the great generals of the ancient world, Alexander was surely the greatest. He possessed an almost clairvoyant insight into strategy and was a consummately resourceful tactician. Like Napoleon, he believed in swiftness of movement, but he could be patient too, as he showed in his long siege of the formidable fortress of Tyre.

He was enormously skillful at dealing with un-

familiar tactics of warfare, such as the use of chariots armed with scythes, elephants deployed in
battle, and evasive, encircling movements by nomad
horsemen. Sometimes he got unexpected help from
the enemy. Darius, who was cruel as well as cow-
ardly, treated prisoners with a harshness that em-
bittered the Macedonian soldiers. In two major
battles, at Issus in 333 B.C. and Gaugamela in 331
B.C., Darius fled from the field. With these two
victories Alexander broke the main Persian resistance and in the autumn of 331 B.C. he entered
Babylon, the winter capital of the Persian kings. In
December of the same year he entered the summer
capital at Susa. From Susa he went on to the ceremonial capital at Persepolis. Here he collected a
treasure so vast, says Plutarch, that it took 20,000
mules and 5,000 camels to remove it. Before leaving
Persepolis, Alexander burned the huge palace of
the Great King for reasons that have never been
clear. Possibly it was a whim, possibly he did it
in a fit of drunken excitement, or possibly he did
it to signify that the Persian invasion of Greece
had at last been avenged.

Alexander already considered himself King of
Persia, but his right to the throne was in question
as long as Darius was still at large. In the summer
of 330 B.C., Alexander marched north in pursuit of
him. He had almost caught up with his quarry
when the Persian leader was suddenly slain by his
own men, finally brought to rebellion by their long
resentment of his mismanagement of the Persian
defense. Alexander came upon Darius' body near
Hecatompylos, and ordered it sent back to Persepolis for burial in the royal cemetery of the Achaemenid kings. Now, at last, Alexander was officially
the Great King of Persia. In his new role he headed
east to take possession of the remaining Persian
provinces. After two years he reached and subdued
Bactria and Sogdiana; he now controlled all the
lands that had belonged to Darius.

Alexander's goal at the start of the Persian invasion was the destruction of the Persian army.
If he thought of the Empire at all, he thought of
it simply as a source of wealth. Consequently he
did little to establish his control beyond setting
up military garrisons. But as he took over more
and more territory, he saw that he could not hold
the Empire without also governing it, and that
to govern it effectively he had to merge it with
the Greek world. He proved to be as skillful at
statecraft as he was at military matters.

Since his main concern was to keep the Empire
functioning, Alexander tolerated many local religious and social customs. He even, to some extent,
permitted each country to keep its national institutions. At the same time he introduced a number of
Hellenic ideas. The most important one was that
of the Greek city-state. He was liberal with his
name and among the cities he founded were no
fewer than 16 Alexandrias. Most of them were built
from the foundation up. The first and most famous
one was the Egyptian city which became, a century
later, the center of the Hellenistic world.

As his Empire grew Alexander saw that Asia
could not be administered simply as a colony of
Greece. Somehow he had to bring Persians and
Greeks together into a single unit. In 327 B.C.,
partly for political reasons, but perhaps also for
love, he married a Sogdian Princess, Roxane. Alexander does not seem to have cared much for wom-
en. Plutarch writes that "he was wont to say that
sleep and the act of generation chiefly made him
sensible that he was mortal; as much as to say,
that weariness and pleasure proceed from the same
frailty and imbecility of human nature." Three
years after his marriage to Roxane, he married the
elder daughter of Darius in a purely political union.
This wedding was a communal affair: at the same
time, on Alexander's order, 80 of his top-ranking
officers married 80 Persian girls of noble birth.

Further to consolidate his Empire Alexander drafted Persian cavalry into his own army and ordered 30,000 Persian boys to be trained in Macedonian combat techniques. He adopted Persian dress for himself and for a time even tried to get his soldiers to follow the Persian custom of prostration before the King. But his Macedonian captains were affronted by this. They felt that it implied worship, and they did not think that Alexander was a god.

Once Alexander called together his Persian and Macedonian captains and urged them to regard the whole world as their home and all good men as their brothers. This was not a plea for the brotherhood of man. That idea Alexander left to the philosophers of the next generation, who made it a cardinal point of their teaching. His own vision of brotherhood was inspired by simple political expediency: he saw that he could not hold the Empire without granting its people some rights and powers. He wanted his Persian captains to feel that they were the equals of the Macedonians and wanted the Macedonians to accept this equality.

Possibly it was also political expediency that prompted Alexander to announce that he wished to be regarded as a representative of the gods. Quasi-divinity gave him a status that transcended his dual role as leader of the Greeks and King of Persia. The Persians agreed to his wish willingly enough; they were accustomed to associating kings with gods. The Greeks, however, scoffed at the idea. Although they sometimes recognized men as gods, it was almost unheard of for a man to deify himself. Divinity was an honor bestowed on a man by others.

Most of Alexander's ideas for consolidating the Greek and Persian peoples made little impression on his Macedonian companions. They were soldiers, not political scientists. His concept of empire did not fit their own crude ambitions and they had no sympathy for his desire to govern responsibly.

They felt that he was setting himself above them, spoiling the old sense of comradeship-in-arms which had once characterized the Macedonian army. They resented his treatment of the Persians as their equals, which obliterated the age-old distinctions between Greeks and barbarians. They were dismayed when he put Greeks under the command of Persians, and made Persians governors. More than once, Alexander was faced with conspiracy. He could never be sure that forces left behind to govern occupied cities would not revolt. He could never rule out the danger of assassination. And yet he held his enormous Empire together.

After he had taken over the provinces of Bactria and Sogdiana, completing his conquest of the Persian Empire, Alexander turned south and headed into India. Nearly two centuries before, in the reign of Darius I, the Persian Empire had included part of that subcontinent. Determined to recapture it, Alexander crossed the Hindu Kush mountains, followed the Kabul River down to the Indus River and crossed overland to the Hydaspes River. At the Hydaspes, near a place now called Jhelum, he fought one of the most difficult battles of his entire career. His opponent was the Indian King, Porus, whose army was several times larger than Alexander's and superbly trained. It included war elephants, and the huge beasts reduced Alexander's striking power because his horses would not go near them. By feinting a series of attacks and finally attacking from an unexpected quarter, Alexander defeated Porus. One of the casualties of battle, however, was his own horse, Bucephalus. Alexander had earned him as a boy of 12 by riding him when no one else could. He founded a city in his memory on the site of the battle, naming it Bucephala.

From the Hydaspes Alexander advanced deeper into India. Like most men of his time he believed that the Indian continent was a small peninsula jutting eastward, and that its uttermost extremity was washed by the body of water, called simply Ocean, that encircled the world. He expected to reach Ocean and explore it as the climax of his long campaign. With this in mind he had brought with him rowers and shipwrights from Phoenicia, Cyprus, Caria and Egypt, and had even chosen his admiral, a boyhood friend named Nearchus. But his troops had other ideas. They could see the point of the Persian campaigns, but not of an invasion of India. They had heard rumors of vast deserts and fierce warriors and great armies of elephants lying ahead. Besides, they were tired and yearned for home. They refused to march.

Alexander waited three days for them to change their minds. When he was convinced that they would not, he agreed to start home. On the banks of the River Hyphasis, he erected 12 altars to the gods of Olympus, in gratitude for granting him so many victories and leading him within reach of the world's end. Then he divided his troops, sending one group back by ship, under Nearchus, with instructions to explore the coastline of the Indian Ocean and the Persian Gulf. A second group went back by land, following a northerly route. The rest of the army, under Alexander, returned through the southern regions of what are now Baluchistan and Iran. Much of this route lay through scorching desert. The heat was so intense that the army had to march at night. For a stretch of 200 miles, the guides lost their way. Food supplies ran low and the baggage animals had to be slaughtered. Alexander brought his army through and shared its hardships. He sent his horse to the rear and went on foot, and refused water when there was not enough for everyone.

In the spring of 323 B.C. he reached Babylon, and began almost at once to regroup his army and plan an invasion of Arabia. But in June a fever struck him. The efforts and privations of the journey had undermined his hitherto magnificent

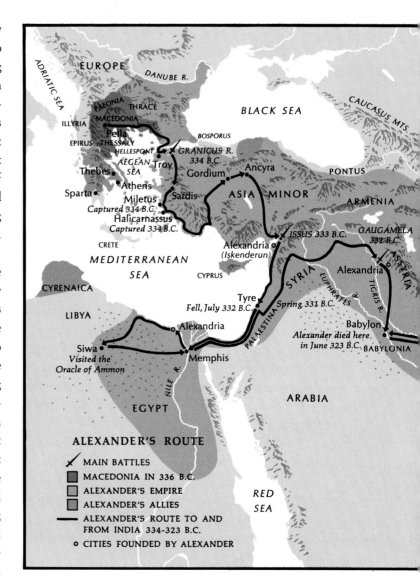

THE STEPS OF A MIGHTY CONQUEROR

THE EPOCHAL CAMPAIGN *that Alexander began in 334 B.C. and that took him 11 years to complete is traced on the map above. (On entering Asia he made a personal detour from his principal aim: he left the army to visit Troy, legendary scene of the exploits of his hero, Achilles.) He began with a mixed Macedonian-Greek force of 30,000 infantrymen and 5,000 cavalry, of which the most important were the 2,000 "Companions." The infantry included heavily armed spear and shield carriers, and lightly armed javelin throwers and archers. There was also a siege train equipped with portable towers and rams on wheels.*

Map labels:
ARAL SEA
CASPIAN SEA
JAXARTES R.
FERGANA
SOGDIANA
Maracanda (Samarkand)
Alexandria Eschata (Leninabad)
Bokhara
Winter 328-327 B.C.
327 B.C.
HINDU KUSH MTS.
Bactra-Zariaspa
BACTRIA
BADAKHSHAN
Alexandria ad Caucasum
MEDIA
Hecatompylos
Darius died near here in 330 B.C.
Ecbatana
PARTHIA
Alexandria Arion (Herat)
ARIA
AFGHANISTAN
Alexandria (Ghazni)
GANDHARA
KABUL R.
HYDASPES R. 326 B.C.
Nicaea
Spring 330 B.C.
ARACHOSIA
HYDRAOTIS R. 325 B.C.
HYPHASIS R.
Susa
IRAN
Spring 329 B.C.
Alexandria Arachosiae (Kandahar)
Alexander wounded
Persepolis
PERSIS
BALUCHISTAN
Alexandria (Golashkerd)
BALUCHISTAN DESERT
Alexandria
Alexandria Opiana (Uch)
INDIA
INDUS R.
Autumn and winter 325 B.C.
PERSIAN GULF
Pattala
July 325 B.C.
INDIAN OCEAN
N

SCALE
0   100   200   300 Miles

health. He grew rapidly worse, and soon could no longer speak. One by one his captains filed past his bed; he was unable to do more than lift his hand and make a sign with his eyes. On the 13th of June, 323 B.C., not yet 33 years old, he died.

With his death the political structure of his Empire disintegrated almost immediately. The Indian conquests reverted to their own rulers, and Alexander's generals, grabbing for power, soon divided what was left. One, named Seleucus, seized most of Persia and formed the Seleucid Empire; another, Ptolemy, established the dynasty of the Ptolemies in Egypt; and a third, Antigonus, became King of Macedon. In Greece the League of Corinth fell apart. Athens and Sparta were again independent city-states, while most of the other states joined in one of two new alliances, the Aetolian and Achaean Leagues, neither of which had much authority or influence beyond its own membership.

Alexander's successors in Asia claimed to carry on his rule, and they followed at least some of his patterns. They modeled their cities on the Greek city-state and adopted the Greek language as the lingua franca of their world. They even appropriated Alexander's titles and attributes, and stamped their coins with his image.

In Bactria and India petty rulers for many centuries claimed to be his direct descendants. The Indian King Chandragupta saw in Alexander's success the possibility of uniting India under a single monarchy. The Mirs of Badakhshan believed that their horses were descended from Alexander's horse, Bucephalus. Greek art influenced the art of all of western Asia and left an enduring mark on the sculpture of the Gandhara school in India. Greek design infiltrated Persian design, and from there moved to the Far East. Objects showing Greek influence have been found at the western end of the Great Wall of China. Several hundred years after Alexander's death, Roman legions pushing into the eastern Mediterranean and Asia found the residue of his system still working and learned from it some of the arts of ruling an empire.

Alexander himself was barely dead when he became the subject of a romantic legend. The story of his life was retold throughout the inhabited world. For scope and variety it has almost no parallel. There are more than 80 versions, written in 24 languages and ranging from Britain to Malaya. In one version his conquests take him westward to Rome and Carthage, and then through the Pillars of Heracles to the Western Ocean. In another he is made the ruler of a world-kingdom that, according to Biblical prophecy, precedes the coming of a Messiah. The Persian tale has him going on from India to cross Tibet, part of China and part of Russia, until he comes to the Land of Darkness. As Iskander, "the two-horned," he became one of the legendary heroes of Islam and was still part of Islamic folklore when Napoleon invaded Egypt. Bedouin tribesmen thought that Napoleon was Iskander reincarnated.

Alexander's career made a splendid sunset to the long day of classical Greece, but it was nonetheless a sunset. The Greeks had achieved their marvelous successes by concentrating their powers on certain accepted ends, and by assuming that no other people could do what they did. Alexander began this way, too. Like the Greeks he loved action and lived for action above everything. Just as Homer's Achilles preferred a short and glorious life to a long and inglorious one, so Alexander was driven by his own temperament to a similar destiny. He embodied the Greek spirit, with its love of effort, its capacity for improvisation, its adaptation of ideals to reality, its unconquerable urge to realize a full life for the individual.

After Alexander, Greece was never the same. Politically it maintained its independence, but it never regained its former power and after two centuries was conquered by Rome. Culturally its influence after Alexander was wider than it had ever been, but it was also more diffuse and less homogeneous. The opening of Asia to Greek trade inevitably broadened the Greeks' outlook—and at the same time introduced essentially alien ideas into their cultural life. Classical Hellenism was modified by Asian influences and became Hellenistic. In this form Greece influenced Rome, Egypt and large areas of Asia, but Greek civilization had lost the brilliance and zest of its morning and noon.

The long process which began in the Dark Age of Ionia and reached its heyday in Periclean Athens first began to decline with the Peloponnesian War. The inspired confidence which had carried Greece from one success to another was in the end its undoing. Athenians, maintaining in their democracy all the elegances and virtues of an aristocratic society, thought that nobody could withstand them. For a time events seemed to prove them right. But Athens attempted too much, and so had to fail. With its failure, the rest of Greece failed too. The fine intelligence began to turn against itself; the old fortitude was broken; the creative impulse narrowed its field of endeavor.

If ever a people changed the face of the world, it was the Greeks of the Sixth and Fifth Centuries B.C. Without them we should indeed be different from what we are, certainly much poorer in the gifts of the spirit and the imagination. They exploited the whole range of human nature and created an ideal of man that had never existed in so full a form before and was perhaps never to be realized so fully again. There was almost no sphere of life which the Greeks did not touch and transform, no accomplishment they attempted that they did not perform at the highest level. Other peoples may have had longer histories, but none left so rich a record of what man can do when he believes in himself and in the world into which he is born.

A CAVALRYMAN IN BATTLE *appears on a coin issued by Macedonia's dependency, Paeonia. Paeonia furnished contingents of horsemen to the armies with which Alexander established the Hellenistic world.*

AFTERMATH OF EMPIRE

Alexander multiplied the Greek world fourfold—and paradoxically made the earth a smaller place. When his troops reached India, they effectively ended Persian control of the profitable trade routes to the Orient. Alexander put into circulation the gold hoard heaped up by Darius, and thus further stimulated international trade. He instituted a uniform coinage for his vast domain, thus freeing commerce from ancient regional restrictions. The Greeks came from their tiny city-states to share in the new affluence. In the 300 years that followed Alexander's death in 323 B.C., they created a different era—the Hellenistic age —that extended the influence of that remarkable man for many more centuries.

A SHIFT TO REALISM IN ART

Greek art in the Hellenistic period changed with the changing character of the people. The detachment of classical sculpture gave way to an exploration of human emotions that utilized a greater knowledge of anatomy and a wider range of acceptable subject matter. Art, once a religious exercise, became big business. The new cities in Egypt and Syria wanted statues for their temples and streets. Not only kings and generals but rich merchants bought marble replicas of themselves. Athens boomed on the profits of its sculpture. Athenian sculptors turned out both original work and fair copies of old statues. Boatloads of artwork were shipped to all parts of the Mediterranean. Eventually factories were set up near the quarries to turn out statues wholesale. Even so, supply never kept up with demand.

AN OLD WOMAN *is a Roman copy of a Hellenistic work showing a very real and wrinkled woman who is finding release from her cares in a bout of drinking. Classical sculpture had preferred to portray beautiful young women.*

LAOCOÖN AND HIS SONS, *a powerful study of terror, was done by three sculptors. The family is shown in the death grip of serpents sent by the gods as punishment after Laocoön urged the Trojans not to touch the wooden horse.*

A STUMP OF A COLUMN *from the temple of Apollo at Didyma shows the search for the ornate in Hellenistic architecture. In place of a severe Ionic base, there is a foundation of intricate carvings.*

NEW, ORNATE CITIES

No matter where they were situated, the new cities of the Hellenistic world were Greek—in architecture, language, law and entertainment. Palmyra, to cite one example, was transformed from a caravan stop in arid central Syria into a thriving city with a marketplace, a senate, a theater, shops and fine dwellings. Here, as elsewhere in Hellenistic cities, the austerity of Doric and Ionic was replaced by the more elaborate Corinthian style. These towns, laid out in carefully planned grids wherever the terrain permitted, had more libraries, parks, gardens and palaces than the cities of Greece. They had great temples too, but often to gods strange to Greece. In the twilight of classical Greece, some Greeks turned to philosophy, others to Egyptian and Near Eastern deities—housed in temples of Greek design.

A FUSION OF STYLES *on a sarcophagus of the Second Century A.D. combines a Greek treatment of face and figure with an Eastern sumptuousness in the sculptured wreaths and bunches of grapes.*

A STREET IN PALMYRA *is lined with columns that in classical Greece might have been considered too grand for anything less than an important temple.*

ALEXANDER'S CAMPING GROUND *at Bactra, in modern Afghanistan, is near a camel caravan route. He spent two winters there en route to India.*

GREECE IN ASIA

The long reach of Hellenistic influence is nowhere more dramatically evident than in ancient India. Greeks ruled there only intermittently, first under Alexander, then again a century later. But in Gandhara—a region now in Pakistan and Afghanistan —a school of religious art arose that was Hellenistic in technique and style. It flourished for about seven centuries. It is possible that the first representation of the Lord Buddha in human form arose in this school. It was a figure like the one opposite, modeled on the Greek god Apollo. Earlier Buddhists thought it repugnant to depict the Buddha, but soon the Buddha's image was embedded in the religion.

HANDMAIDENS OF THE QUEEN *in a Gandharan carving are in attendance at the birth of the Buddha. The modeling of the costumes echoes the skillful handling of draperies by Greek sculptors.*

A HEAD OF BUDDHA, *made in Gandhara, is a modified head of Apollo topped by the bump traditionally said to contain the Buddha's special brain. The bump is covered with a topknot.*

171

A SHATTERED ATHENA, *the proud patron of the most civilized aspects of Greek life, lies on the ground (left). The work, which was discovered at Side in southern Turkey, was part of a Hellenistic theater's decoration.*

INTACT COLUMNS *of the ruined Temple of the Olympian Zeus in Athens, the largest Hellenistic shrine built in European Greece, stand today as soaring testaments to the aspiration that filled the hearts of Greeks.*

FINAL ACTS ON A CHANGING STAGE

Athens, the center of classical Greece's most gloriously vibrant days, found a different role in the Hellenistic world. No longer a sea power, its destiny was decided at times by Macedonia, at other times by Egypt. Athens' intellectual leadership was challenged by Alexandria, with its new Museum and its large library. Nevertheless, Athens was still revered as the fount of Greek thought and learning. There Philemon wrote his plays. The school of Aristotle flourished under Theophrastus. Zeno and

Epicurus taught their differing philosophies to new generations. Hellenistic kings beautified Athens with new buildings. The leading families of Egypt, Syria and Macedonia, and later the upstarts from Rome, sent their children to be educated at Athens. Not until Justinian closed the Athenian schools 500 years after the birth of Christ did the statues begin to fall, the city to crumble. But by then Athens was more than a city. It had become the expression of an intellectual freedom that will never die.

"Future ages will wonder at us,

as the present age wonders at us now"

CAPE SUNIUM

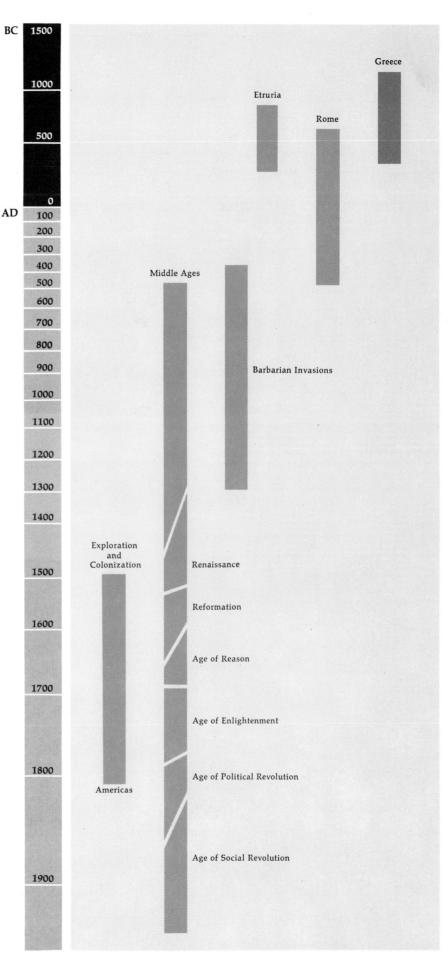

GREAT AGES
OF WESTERN
CIVILIZATION

The chart at right is designed to show the duration of the Greek culture that forms the subject matter of this volume, and to relate this culture to other cultures of the Western world that are considered in one major group of volumes of this series. A comprehensive world chronology—from which this chart is excerpted—appears in the introductory booklet to this series. Comparison of the chart seen here with the world chronology will relate the great ages of Western civilization to important cultures in other parts of the world, some of which are the subject of other volumes in the series.

On the next two pages is a table of the important events which took place in Greece during the period covered by this book.

CHRONOLOGY: A listing of events significant in the history of ancient Greece

Thought and Culture

- **c. 776** The first Olympic Games are held
- **c. 750** Music is developed in Greek Asia. Oriental influences enter Greek art
- **c. 750-700** Homer's epic poems, the *Iliad* and the *Odyssey*, are composed

- **c. 705** Greek architects begin building in stone
- **c. 700** The poet Hesiod flourishes
- **c. 700** Human figures appear as main subjects in pottery painting
- **c. 675** The poet Archilochus flourishes in Paros
- **c. 650** Large free-standing sculpture is evolved
- **c. 630** The poet Alcman flourishes in Sparta

- **c. 600** Attic black-figured style in pottery is developed
- **c. 600** Lyric poetry reaches its height: poets Sappho and Alcaeus flourish at Lesbos
- **c. 580** Philosophy and science begin with the teachings of Thales and Anaximander

- **c. 550** Doric architecture is standardized. Ionic influences appear in the architecture of mainland Greece and the West
- **c. 534** Thespis, the reputed founder of Greek tragedy, is the first victor at Athens' drama festival
- **c. 530** The mathematician Pythagoras establishes a religious fraternity at Croton
- **c. 525** The Attic red-figured style in pottery is developed
- **c. 520** The poet Simonides of Ceos and the philosopher Xenophanes are at their peak

- **c. 500** The philosopher Heraclitus teaches at Ephesus in Asia Minor

- **484** Aeschylus wins his first victory at Athens' drama festival

- **480** The Acropolis is destroyed by the Persians

- **c. 480-445** The sculptor Myron is at work in Athens

B.C.

1200	DARK AGE
800	GEOMETRIC ART
	ARISTOCRATIC AGE
600	ARCHAIC ART
	AGE OF ATHENIAN TYRANTS
500	CONFLICT WITH PERSIA

Politics and Society

- **c. 1200** The Dorians invade Greece, destroying the Mycenaean civilization
- **c. 1130** Iron comes into general use for weapons and tools
- **c. 1100** The Greeks begin colonization on the Ionian coast of Asia Minor

- **c. 750** Greek colonies are planted in Italy

- **c. 700** Athens combines with the towns of Attica to form a single political unit
- **c. 683** An aristocratic republic, ruled by archons elected for one-year terms, is fully established in Athens

- **621** Draco issues his severe legal code
- **c. 610** The use of coined money spreads on mainland Greece
- **594** Solon initiates social and constitutional reform in Athens

- **561** The tyrant Peisistratus seizes power in Athens

- **527** Peisistratus is succeeded by his sons, Hippias and Hipparchus
- **520** Persia completes its domination of Ionia
- **514** Hipparchus, youngest son of the tyrant Peisistratus, is murdered
- **510** Hippias, eldest son of Peisistratus, is overthrown
- **507** Athenian democracy is restored and broadened by Cleisthenes

- **499** The Ionian Greeks revolt against Persian rule
- **494** The Ionian revolt collapses
- **493** Themistocles, elected archon of Athens, starts fortifying the harbor at Piraeus
- **490** Darius of Persia launches an attack on mainland Greece, starting the Persian Wars. The Persians are repelled in the Battle of Marathon
- **483** A rich silver strike at Mount Laurium provides Athens with funds to expand its fleet
- **481** The Greek states, under Sparta's leadership, meet to plan a united effort against the Persians
- **480** The Greeks are crushed at Thermopylae, then win a victory at Salamis
- **479** The last major battles of the war, Plataea and Mycale, end in defeat for Persia

- **478-477** Athens leads in forming the Delian League of Greek states

Cultural and artistic events

472 Aeschylus' play *The Persians* is produced
468 The dramatist Sophocles introduces the use of more than two actors in tragedy
468 The first drama contest between Sophocles and Aeschylus is won by Sophocles
467 Aeschylus' *Seven against Thebes* is presented
462 The philosopher Anaxagoras comes to Athens
c. 460 The physician Hippocrates is born
458 Aeschylus' *Oresteia* is produced
c. 456 The Temple of Zeus at Olympia is completed
455 Euripides' first tragedy is performed

447 Ictinus and Callicrates design and begin building the Parthenon
446 The poet Pindar writes the last of his odes still extant
444 Protagoras, a Sophist, draws up laws for the new colony of Thurii
442 or 441 Sophocles' *Antigone* is produced
438 Phidias' statue *Athena Parthenos* is dedicated
437 The Propylaea (monumental gateway to Acropolis) is begun
432 Phidias completes his work on the Parthenon friezes
431 Euripides' tragedy *Medea* is produced
429 or 427 Sophocles' tragedy *Oedipus Rex* is produced
424 The historian Thucydides is appointed an Athenian general
423 Aristophanes' *The Clouds* is presented

c. 415 Euripides' *Trojan Women* is staged
414 Aristophanes' comedy *The Birds* is produced
413 Euripides' *Electra* is presented
411 The production of Aristophanes' *Lysistrata*
409-406 The Erectheum is completed on the Acropolis
405 Aristophanes' *The Frogs* is presented

401 Sophocles' *Oedipus at Colonus* is produced
401 The historian Xenophon conducts the retreat from Cunaxa
399 Socrates, tried and condemned to death, dies by drinking hemlock
c. 385 Plato starts teaching at Athens
c. 380 Isocrates, a speech-writer, urges the unity of Greece in his *Panegyricus*

c. 350 The sculptor Praxiteles flourishes
343 Aristotle becomes a tutor to Alexander of Macedonia

335 Aristotle founds a school in Athens

330 Statues of Aeschylus, Euripides and Sophocles are erected in the new Theatre of Dionysus at Athens

---

450   **400**   **350**

RISE OF ATHENIAN EMPIRE | PELOPONNESIAN WAR | SUPREMACY OF SPARTA | RISE OF MACEDONIAN EMPIRE

Political and military events

468 The Delian League destroys the new Persian fleet
462-461 Pericles, with the statesman Ephialtes, brings democratic reforms to Athens
459 Athens wins Megara away from Sparta. The rivalry between Sparta and Athens increases
457 The Long Walls are built to protect Athens
457 Athens conquers Boeotia
454-3 The treasury of the Delian League is transferred from Delos to Athens, signaling Athenian dominance
451 Athenian citizenship is restricted. Pay for jurors is introduced
c. 448 The Athenian Empire is fully established
447 The Athenian defeat at Coronea begins the decline of the Empire
445 The Thirty Years' Peace is declared between Athens and Sparta

431 The Peloponnesian War breaks out between Sparta and Athens
429 Pericles dies
423 War is interrupted by a one-year armistice
422 The Athenians are defeated at Amphipolis, in Thrace. Peace negotiations open
421 Temporary peace is declared between Athens and Sparta
419 Athens renews the war
418 Athens is defeated at the Battle of Mantinea
415 The Athenian fleet under Alcibiades sails against Syracuse in Sicily. Alcibiades defects to Sparta
413 The naval battle at Syracuse ends in the defeat of Athens
405 The Athenian fleet is destroyed at Aegospotami, in Thrace
404 Athens surrenders to Sparta

404-371 Sparta sporadically fights other Greek states and Persia
382 The Spartans seize the citadel of Thebes
379-8 The Spartans are expelled from Thebes
378 Sparta and Thebes form an alliance
371 Sparta is defeated by its former ally Thebes

359 Philip II takes the throne of Macedonia and expands his realm
351 Demosthenes arouses the Athenians against Philip
338 Philip defeats Athens and its allies at Chaeronea and becomes the supreme power in Greece
336 Philip is assassinated. His son Alexander succeeds him
335 Alexander razes Thebes and extends Macedonian rule
334 Alexander launches an expedition against Persia, wins the Battle of the River Granicus
333 The Battle of Issus is fought
331 Alexander is victorious at the Battle of Gaugamela
330 Alexander enters Persepolis; with Persian power smashed, he moves farther into Asia
323 Alexander dies in Babylon. His successors begin to carve up his empire

THE OLYMPIAN FAMILY

In the beginning, according to Greek belief, there was a great void called Chaos. From Chaos ultimately issued forth the Elder Gods, or Titans, led by Cronos. Cronos' son Zeus led the next generation of deities—the Olympians—the gods worshiped by the Greeks through the Golden Age of their history. Listed here are the chief Olympians.

ARTEMIS, *virgin goddess of the moon, twin sister of Apollo, mighty huntress and "rainer of arrows," was the guardian of cities, of young animals and of women of all ages. To her women prayed for easy childbirth and she was the midwife at the birth of her own twin brother, Apollo. She could be harsh: she blocked the passage of the Greek army to Troy because Agamemnon boasted he was a better shot than she was, and demanded the sacrifice of his daughter. But some say she spared the girl's life.*

ZEUS, *ruler of Mount Olympus, king of gods and men, god of the weather, sixth child of Cronos and his wife Rhea, was to have been eaten by his father, as were his brothers and sisters. But his mother hid him and fed Cronos a stone instead. Grown up, Zeus then fed Cronos an emetic and he coughed up his sons and daughters. They joined Zeus against the elder gods. Using lightning stolen from their elders, the rebel children won the battle and the universe.*

worshiped her, sprang full grown from the forehead of Zeus. In earliest times Athena was depicted as a young girl, but as Athens, her favorite city, aged, so did the goddess. Eventually she was shown as a matronly figure, under whose protection flourished all that was most valued in civilized Athens: the intellect, and the gentle arts of living. She was said to have invented the flute, but in womanly fashion she scorned this instrument after seeing how disfigured her face looked when she puffed out her cheeks to blow on it. Although she helped the Greeks win at Troy, she took vengeance on those heroes who failed to pay her appropriate homage. She established the rule of law, even the concept of mercy, in the trial that freed Orestes from the dread Furies after he had murdered his mother at Apollo's orders. Some say that her gift of the olive tree to mankind won her the devotion of Athens.

APOLLO, *god of the sun and patron of truth, archery, music, medicine and prophecy, was the most majestic of the Olympians. This son of Zeus is associated with the basic Greek precepts: "Know thyself" and "Nothing in excess." In Delphi he established the oracle, an order of prophets that gave advice to Greece, both good and bad, and prophecies, both clear and murky.*

PALLAS ATHENA, *virgin patron of the household crafts, goddess of wisdom and protectress in war of those who*

APHRODITE, *the goddess of love and beauty, presided, the poet Hesiod said, over "girlish babble, and tricks: sweet rapture, embraces and caresses." Wherever she walked flowers sprang up, and sparrows and doves flew about her. To Ares, her lover, she bore several children, among them Fear and Terror. But she had the power to beguile even wise gods and often placed temptation in the path of Zeus, making him forget "the love of Hera, his sister and his bride."*

guardian of wayfarers, celebrated on the day he was born by stealing Apollo's cattle. He confused his pursuers with an ingeniously devised false trail. Caught, he protested that he was too young for stealing. Perhaps with tongue in cheek, this trickster was named god not only of commerce and the market-place, but of orators and writers as well.

HERA, protectress of marriage, married women, children and the home, was both Zeus's wife and his sister, one of those coughed up by Cronos. Some tales say that Zeus courted her for 300 years before she would marry him. Hera wanders through the stories of the gods, always a betrayed wife, torturing girls because Zeus loved them.

DEMETER, goddess of crops, giver of grain and fruit, withheld her gifts when Zeus permitted Hades to carry off her daughter Persephone to the underworld. Famine spread until a compromise could be reached; Persephone would spend only one third of the year in the underworld. Then Demeter relented, and crops flourished anew.

HERMES, Zeus's son and mes-senger to mortals, protector of flocks and cattle, of thieves and mischief-makers, and

POSEIDON, god of the sea and earthquakes, and giver of horses to man, had a palace built "of gleaming gold," Homer says, deep in the Aegean Sea. The Greeks were thankful for the horse but they were always wary of the treacherous seas. And so they prayed to Poseidon to "be kindly in heart and help those who voyage in ships."

DIONYSUS, god of the vine and fertility, of the joyous life and hospital-ity was the son of Zeus by a mortal mother. Jealous Hera destroyed his mother and drove him mad. He wandered the earth accompa-nied by satyrs and maenads. A symbol of revelry, he gave Greece the gift of wine—at times man's blessing, at others his ruin.

ARES, god of war, appropriate-ly symbolized by the vulture, was detested by Zeus and Hera, his mother and father, but was liked by Hades, for the wars Ares started increased the population of the un-derworld. Ares embarrassed the other gods when he and Aphrodite were caught in a rendezvous by her husband, Hephaestus, who trapped the lovers with a nearly invis-ible net. But Ares, although a persistent war-rior, was not a very successful one. He was captured by giants and wounded thrice by Heracles and once by Diomedes. As a sym-bol of war, of its evil, its suffering and its sorrow, he was held in awe by the Greeks but he was never an object of adoration.

HEPHAESTUS, god of fire and artisans, was, according to one legend, ex-pelled from Olympus by his own mother, Hera, in disgust at his lameness. From his forges came many marvels, among them the first mortal woman, Pandora, into whom the gods breathed life. On Olympus he built himself a magnificent, shining, bronze pal-ace staffed by many mechanical servants. Athens, a discerning city in matters of work-manship, held him in the highest esteem.

A GALLERY OF HEROES

The heroes of Greek mythology, as distinguished from the gods, were mortals, but special mortals, some of whom claimed descent from the gods; their feats were chronicled in tales and depicted in works of art that expressed Greek views of life and human conduct. To this day authors, artists and composers find inspiration in stories of the heroes. Highlights from the lives of some of the most famous of them follow.

OEDIPUS, *journeying to Thebes, killed an old man in a scuffle. He then challenged the Sphinx, a monster which ate all passersby who could not solve this riddle: What creature goes on four feet in the morning, two at noonday and three in the evening? Oedipus' correct answer: Man, who first crawls, then walks, finally must use a cane. Oedipus was rewarded with the hand of Jocasta, widowed Queen of Thebes. It had been prophesied that Oedipus would murder his father and marry his mother, and the prophecy had now come true—for Jocasta was his mother, and the man he had slain was her former husband and Oedipus' father. When Jocasta and Oedipus discovered their horrible sin, she killed herself. Oedipus put out his eyes and wandered throughout Greece, prey to the Furies. Athens finally sheltered him and he died there, promising that his body would save the city from harm.*

IO *was loved by Zeus; he turned her into a heifer to hide her from his wife Hera. Hera, undeceived, put the calf under the guard of hundred-eyed Argus. Io escaped, but Hera pursued her with a gadfly until Zeus restored her to human form. Later they had a son who started the line of Heracles.*

gave thanks for their deliverance and heard a voice ordering them to throw the bones of their mother over their shoulders. At first they refused. Then Deucalion realized the earth was their mother and her bones were stones. The boulders they threw turned into human beings who repopulated the world.

HERACLES *was given 12 tasks to complete in atonement for a crime committed by his father. In turn Heracles: (1) choked to death the "invulnerable" lion of Nemea; (2) killed the nine-headed Hydra; (3) captured a golden-horned stag after chasing it for a year; (4) trapped a great boar by running it to exhaustion; (5) diverted two rivers to flush out the befouled Augean stables; (6) drove away the voracious Stymphalian birds and, as they flew up, shot them down with his bow and arrow; (7) captured the savage bull of Minos; (8) ensnared the man-eating mares of Diomedes; (9) asked for and got the girdle of Hippolyta, Queen of the Amazons; (10) stole the cattle of Geryon, a three-bodied monster and, in the process, set up the Pillars of Heracles (now Gibraltar and Ceuta); (11) held up the sky while he sent Atlas to find the golden apples of the Hesperides, then tricked Atlas into resuming the burden of the heavens; (12) captured Cerberus, the three-headed dog of Hades.*

PERSEUS, *as a child, was cast into the sea by his grandfather, who was attempting to forestall the prophecy that the boy would one day kill him. Perseus was rescued and when he grew up went to the land of the Gorgons. These creatures with wings, body scales, and hair made of twisting snakes, were so ugly that those who looked upon them turned to stone. With the help of the gods Perseus killed Medusa, one of the Gorgons, and carried away her head. He freed Andromeda, a princess threatened by a man-eating sea serpent, and wed her. Next he turned his mother's insistent suitor to stone by displaying Medusa's head—and fulfilled the prophecy by accidentally killing his grandfather.*

DEUCALION and PYRRHA, *his wife, were the sole survivors of the flood with which Zeus destroyed a world grown wicked. The pair floated on the waters in a large chest which they had stocked with provisions. As the waters receded the couple*

of the Golden Fleece of a fabled ram. After many adventures—fighting Harpies, skillfully avoiding battle with Amazons—the heroes, called the Argonauts, reached Colchis on the Black Sea. Jason seized the Golden Fleece and fled, accompanied by the sorceress Medea, daughter of the King of Colchis. Jason and Medea lived happily together until Jason left her to marry Creusa. Medea murdered Creusa, then killed her own children and took flight in a chariot drawn by dragons. Jason, distraught, went wandering. One day he lay down in the shade of the "Argo," his old ship, and died when the rotted prow fell on him.

CADMUS, commanded by Apollo to found the city of Thebes, first had to slay the guardian of the site, a dragon which killed all of his companions. To people his city, he planted the dragon's teeth, as instructed by Athena. They sprouted armed men who fought each other until only five remained; with these Cadmus founded Thebes.

BELLEROPHON was ordered to kill the Chimaera, a fire-breathing monster which had a lion's head, the body of a goat and a slithering snake for a tail. Mounted on Pegasus, the winged horse, Bellerophon soared above the Chimaera, weakened her with arrows and finished her off by pouring molten lead down her throat. Later Bellerophon angered the gods by trying to fly on Pegasus to join them in their sacred enclosure on Mount Olympus. But the horse threw him and left him to wander the earth, crippled and blind, and despised by the deities.

EUROPA, sister of Cadmus, was gathering flowers when Zeus appeared to her in the form of a beautiful bull with a silver circle on his brow and horns like the moon's crescent. Persuaded to mount, she crossed the sea on Zeus's back, became his bride and the mother of famous sons, and eventually gave her name to the continent of Europe.

THESEUS, kinsman of Heracles and his rival for heroic honors, cleared the roads into Athens of bandits and penetrated the Cretan labyrinth to kill the half-bull, half-human Minotaur. As King of Athens, he fought Thebes, married an Amazon princess and also sailed on the "Argo" in search of the Golden Fleece. He took part with other Argonauts in the Calydonian Hunt for a terrible boar and battled the Centaurs. Ultimately, he united Attica into a single state.

THE HEROES AT TROY: Achilles, greatest of the Greek warriors and of the line of Zeus, was known for his implacable fury. But he learned in battle that "life is all sorrow," and showed a new compassion by allowing his foe, Hector, an honorable burial; Ajax, in valor and beauty second only to Achilles, realized that he had behaved ignobly toward his friends and ended his life; Agamemnon, commander of the Greeks and brother-in-law of Helen, over whom the war was fought, was killed by his own wife Clytaemnestra for having sacrificed their daughter to Artemis; Odysseus, King of Ithaca, and famed for his shrewdness, invented the Trojan Horse that finally won victory for the Greeks.

ATALANTA, most adventurous of women, took part in the heroes' hunt for the Calydonian boar. She offered to marry any of her suitors who could beat her in a foot race; the losers she would kill. Daring Hippomenes won her hand by carrying three golden apples into the race. Whenever Atalanta took the lead, he threw a golden apple in front of her; as she stopped to pick them up, he passed her and so won the race.

JASON and his band of heroes, among them Heracles, Orpheus, Castor and Pollux, sailed in the ship "Argo" in search

GREEKS GREAT AND FAMOUS

Classical Greece produced literally hundreds of men and women who made lasting contributions to Western civilization. Of this number, 62 of the greatest are identified briefly below. In keeping with the Greek ideal of all-around excellence, many were outstanding in several fields, but for convenience each is classified only according to his major activity. Most dates of birth and death are approximate. All of the dates are B.C.

STATESMEN AND LEADERS

ALCIBIADES
(c.450-404)
Gifted Athenian politician-general who averred that "democracy is acknowledged folly." He turned traitor during the Peloponnesian War.

ALEXANDER THE GREAT
(356-323)
Successor to his father, Philip II, King of Macedon. Alexander launched a 13-year career of conquest that spread his Empire—and Greek culture—around the eastern rim of the Mediterranean, through Asia Minor and into India.

CIMON
(c.512-449)
Conservative Athenian politician and a successful commander in the war against Persia.

CLEISTHENES
(Sixth Century)
Brilliant statesman who revolutionized democratic government in Athens.

CLEON
(Fifth Century)
Successor to Pericles as leader of Athens.

EPAMINONDAS
(c.418-362)
Illustrious Theban soldier-statesman who permanently destroyed the power of Sparta.

EPHIALTES
(Fifth Century)
Athenian statesman responsible for major democratic reforms.

LEONIDAS
(Fifth Century)
King of Sparta and heroic commander of the 300 Spartan soldiers who were wiped out by Xerxes' Persians at Thermopylae in 480 B.C.

LYSANDER
(Fifth Century)
Spartan general and statesman who defeated the Athenian fleet at Aegospotami in 405 B.C.

MILTIADES
(c.550-489)
Athenian general, renowned for his victory over the Persians at Marathon in 490 B.C.

NICIAS
(c.470-413)
Prominent statesman-general who led Athens' campaign against the Syracusans in Sicily.

PEISISTRATUS
(c.605-527)
Athenian tyrant who patronized the arts, beautified the city and promoted its power.

PERICLES
(c.495-429)
Statesman, orator and general, considered the greatest of all Athenians. He brought Athens to its peak of power, and, through democratic reforms and public works, transformed the city.

PHILIP II OF MACEDON
(382-336)
King of Macedon, who, with military genius and masterful diplomacy, took control of all the city-states of Greece.

SOLON
(c.640-c.560)
Reformer whose legal code, with its opposition to tyranny and injustice, laid the constitutional foundations of Athenian democracy.

THEMISTOCLES
(c.528-c.462)
Athenian statesman and commander whose advocacy of sea power and national unity made him the chief architect of victory over Persia.

ORATORS AND SOPHISTS

ANTIPHON
(c.480-411)
Politician, professional speech-writer and one of the earliest great Athenian orators.

DEMOSTHENES
(384-322)
Greatest of Greek orators. An implacable opponent of the rising Macedonians, he won fame for his powerful speeches warning Athens against King Philip II of Macedon.

GORGIAS
(c.483-376)
Prose stylist and noted member of the Sophists, a group of professional instructors who taught public speaking and the art of successful living.

ISOCRATES
(436-338)
Influential speech-writer and teacher of several famous orators.

LYSIAS
(c.459-c.380)
Speech-writer noted for his simple, vivid style.

PROTAGORAS
(c.485-c.411)
Earliest and best known of the Sophists.

POETS AND HISTORIANS

AESCHYLUS
(c.525-456)
Oldest of the three Greek masters of tragedy (Aeschylus, Euripides, Sophocles). His works are dignified, sonorous and philosophic.

ALCAEUS
(Sixth Century)
Lyric poet of Mytilene on the island of Lesbos.

ALCMAN
(Seventh Century)
Spartan poet, considered the inventor of love poetry. He wrote in simple meters, with easy charm.

ARCHILOCHUS
(Seventh Century)
Satirical poet much admired for his verbal and metrical originality.

ARISTOPHANES
(c.450-c.385)
Athenian genius of comedy. His plays are high-spirited, endlessly inventive and laced with scathing attacks on his contemporaries.

BACCHYLIDES
(Fifth Century)
Versatile lyric poet noted for his clarity and narrative skill.

EURIPIDES
(c.485-c.406)
Least orthodox and most realistic of the three great tragic playwrights. His plays express his radical views of morality and religion.

HERODOTUS
(c.484-c.424)
Author of a discursive and humane account of the Persian Wars, which is considered the first historical work of Western civilization.

HESIOD (Eighth Century)	Author of *Works and Days*, a poetic account of farm life, and *The Theogony*, a rich collection of religious lore.
HOMER (Eighth Century)	The giant of epic poetry, author of the *Iliad* and *Odyssey*. Almost nothing is known of his life; it is believed that he was a Greek of humble birth who lived in Asia Minor.
MENANDER (c.342-c.291)	Leading exponent of latter-day Greek comedy. He is considered the father of the modern comedy of manners.
PINDAR (518-438)	Supreme Greek lyric poet. His memory was so revered that when Alexander the Great was sacking Thebes he spared Pindar's home.
SAPPHO (Sixth Century)	Poet of Lesbos so admired for her lyricism that the Greeks called her "the Tenth Muse."
SIMONIDES (c.556-468)	Lyric poet of Ceos, famed for his dirges and his elegies in praise of fallen heroes.
SOPHOCLES (c.496-406)	Most perceptive of the great tragic dramatists. His dramas present characters of noble intentions reacting to situations of terrible stress.
THUCYDIDES (c.460-c.400)	Historian famed for his chronicle of the Peloponnesian War, in which he served as a general.
TYRTAEUS (Seventh Century)	Elegiac poet of Sparta. His poems reputedly roused Spartan soldiers to victory after their defeat in the battle of the Boar's Tomb.
XENOPHON (c.430-c.354)	Historian and biographer. His finest work, the *Anabasis*, was based on his experience as a mercenary in a Persian military unit.

ARTISTS AND ARCHITECTS

CALLICRATES (Fifth Century)	Master builder who helped design the Parthenon and the Temple of Athena Nike on the Acropolis.
ICTINUS (Fifth Century)	Chief architect of his day, associated with Pericles' master plan to beautify Athens. With Callicrates he designed the great Parthenon.
LYSIPPUS (Fourth Century)	The favorite sculptor and frequent portraitist of Alexander the Great. His figure studies set two new styles, one emphasizing extreme muscularity, the other featuring elongated bodies.
MYRON (Fifth Century)	Sculptor famed for his bronzes of performing athletes and his realistic statues of animals.
PHIDIAS (c.490-c.417)	Designer of the Parthenon sculptures, considered the greatest artist of the classical period.
POLYCLITUS (Fifth Century)	Sculptor whose statues were said to epitomize the Greek concept of physical perfection.
POLYGNOTUS (Fifth Century)	Realistic painter who introduced such new effects as the rendering of transparent draperies.

PRAXITELES (Fourth Century)	Celebrated Greek sculptor who excelled at representing emotion, with grace and relaxed strength.
SCOPAS (Fourth Century)	Renowned sculptor born in Paros, a leader in portraying strong emotion and vigorous action.

PHILOSOPHERS AND SCIENTISTS

ANAXAGORAS (c.500-c.428)	Philosopher who maintained that a supreme intelligence imposed a purposeful order on the physical world. He believed that matter was composed of an infinite variety of tiny particles.
ANAXIMANDER (610-c.547)	Philosopher-astronomer who held that all matter consisted of an imperishable substance of limitless quantity. He pioneered the conception of the earth as a body suspended in space.
ARISTOTLE (384-322)	Creator of a philosophy as vastly influential as that of his teacher Plato, but opposed to it. Believing that all theory must follow demonstrable fact, he based his system on direct observation and strict logic. His approach made him the father of the modern scientific method.
DEMOCRITUS (c.460-c.370)	Philosopher whose atomic theory declared that all things are composed of invisible and indestructible particles, and of empty space.
EMPEDOCLES (c.493-c.433)	Philosopher who held that matter was composed of four elements—fire, air, water and earth.
HERACLITUS (c.535-c.475)	Thinker who held that the basic condition of life was change and the basic element was fire.
HIPPOCRATES (c.460-c.377)	Famed physician and medical teacher, an early advocate of sound diet and proper hygiene.
PARMENIDES (Fifth Century)	Radical thinker who held that logic—and not sensory experience—was the only criterion of physical truth.
PLATO (c.429-347)	Towering philosopher who, influenced by his teacher, Socrates, believed in the existence of ideas, the greatest of which was goodness. This idealistic system inspired countless later thinkers whose approach was intuitive and subjective.
PYTHAGORAS (Sixth Century)	Mathematician who sought to explain the nature of all things in mathematical terms.
SOCRATES (469-399)	Powerful thinker and teacher, immortalized by his refusal to save his own life at the price of repudiating his beliefs. His great contribution was his serious inquiry into questions of morality.
THALES (c.640-c.546)	Earliest known Western philosopher. He asserted that the physical world was composed of one basic material, a clear liquid.
ZENO OF ELEA (Fifth Century)	A pupil of Parmenides who used his teacher's logical method in an attempt to prove that space and motion are figments of the imagination.

BIBLIOGRAPHY

These books were selected during the preparation of the volume for their interest and authority, and for their usefulness to readers seeking additional information on specific points.

An asterisk (*) marks works available in both hard-cover and paperback editions; a dagger (†) indicates availability only in paperback.

GENERAL HISTORY

*Andrewes, A., *The Greek Tyrants*. Hillary, 1956.
Botsford, G. W., and C. A. Robinson Jr., *Hellenic History* (4th ed.). Macmillan, 1956.
*Burn, A. R., *Pericles and Athens*. Macmillan, 1949.
Burn, A. R., *Persia and the Greeks*. St. Martin's Press, 1962.
Bury, J. B., *A History of Greece*. Modern Library, 1937.
The Cambridge Ancient History, Vol. IV, *The Persian Empire and the West*. Macmillan, 1926.
The Cambridge Ancient History, Vol. V, *Athens 478-401 B.C.* Macmillan, 1927.
Cook, J. M., *The Greeks in Ionia and the East*. Praeger, 1963.
Gomme, A. W., *Greece*. Oxford University Press, 1945.
Hammond, N.G.L., *A History of Greece to 322 B.C.* Oxford University Press, 1959.
Haywood, Richard M., *Ancient Greece and the Near East*. David McKay, 1964.
Herodotus, *The Persian Wars*. Transl. by George Rawlinson (*The Greek Historians*, Vol. I.). Random House, 1942.
†Kitto, H.D.F., *The Greeks*. Penguin Books, 1963.
Payne, Robert, *Ancient Greece*. Norton, 1964.
Plutarch, *The Lives of the Noble Grecians and Romans*. Transl. by John Dryden. Modern Library, 1932.
Robinson, C. A. Jr., *Athens in the Age of Pericles*. University of Oklahoma Press, 1959.
†Rostovtzeff, M., *Greece*. Oxford University Press, 1963.
†Thucydides, *The Peloponnesian War*. Transl. by Rex Warner. Penguin Books, 1961.
Woodhead, A. G., *The Greeks in the West*. Praeger, 1962.
Zimmern, Alfred E., *The Greek Commonwealth*. Modern Library, 1956.

ECONOMICS, SOCIOLOGY AND CULTURE

Bonnard, André, *Greek Civilization*. 3 vols. Macmillan, 1957-1963.
Bowra, C. M., *The Greek Experience*. World Publishing Co., 1957.
Durant, Will, *The Life of Greece*. Simon and Schuster, 1939.
†Hamilton, Edith, *The Greek Way*. Norton, 1930.
Michell, H., *The Economics of Ancient Greece*. Barnes & Noble, 1957.
Payne, Robert, *The Splendor of Greece*. Harper & Row, 1960.
†Stobart, J. C., *The Glory that was Greece* (3rd ed.). Grove Press, 1962.
Toutain, J., *The Economic Life of the Ancient World*. Barnes & Noble, 1952.
Turner, Ralph, *The Great Cultural Traditions*. 2 vols. McGraw-Hill, 1941.
Quennell, Marjorie and C.H.B., *Everyday Things in Ancient Greece*. Putnam, 1954.

ART, ARCHITECTURE AND ARCHEOLOGY

†Arias, Paolo E., and Max Hirmer, *A History of 1000 Years of Greek Vase Painting*. Harry N. Abrams, 1962.
Berve, Helmut, Gottfried Gruben and Max Hirmer, *Greek Temples, Theatres and Shrines*. Harry N. Abrams, 1962.
Bieber, Margarete, *The Sculpture of the Hellenistic Age*. Columbia University Press, 1961.
Dinsmoor, William B., *The Architecture of Ancient Greece*. London, Batsford, 1950.
Gardner, Helen, *Art Through the Ages* (4th ed.). Harcourt, Brace & World, 1959.
Lawrence, A. W., *Greek Architecture*. Penguin Books, 1957.
Lullies, Reinhard, and Max Hirmer, *Greek Sculpture*. Harry N. Abrams, 1960.
MacKendrick, Paul, *The Greek Stones Speak*. St. Martin's Press, 1962.
Richter, Gisela M. A., *Archaic Greek Art*. Oxford University Press, 1949.
Richter, Gisela M. A., *A Handbook of Greek Art*. Phaidon, 1960.
Richter, Gisela M. A., *Sculpture and Sculptors of the Greeks*. Yale University Press, 1950.
Robertson, D. S., *A Handbook of Greek & Roman Architecture*. Cambridge University Press, 1959.

Robertson, Martin, *Greek Painting*. Skira, World Publishing Co., 1959.
Schoder, Raymond V., S.J. *Masterpieces of Greek Art*. New York Graphic Society, 1965.

LITERATURE

*Hadas, Moses, *A History of Greek Literature*. Columbia University Press, 1950.
†Homer, *The Odyssey*. Transl. by W.H.D. Rouse. Mentor Books, 1964.
*Lattimore, Richmond, ed., *Greek Lyrics*. University of Chicago Press, 1960.
Lattimore, Richmond, ed., *The Iliad of Homer*. University of Chicago Press, 1961.
*Lattimore, Richmond, ed., *The Odes of Pindar*. University of Chicago Press, 1947.
†Murray, Gilbert, *The Rise of the Greek Epic*. Oxford University Press, 1960.

THEATER

Bieber, Margarete, *The History of the Greek and Roman Theater*. Princeton University Press, 1961.
Flickinger, Roy C., *The Greek Theater and its Drama*. University of Chicago Press, 1960.
†Kitto, H.D.F., *Greek Tragedy*. Doubleday, 1954.
†Norwood, Gilbert, *Greek Comedy*. Hill & Wang, 1963.
†Norwood, Gilbert, *Greek Tragedy*. Hill & Wang, 1960.
Oates, Whitney J., and Eugene O'Neill Jr., eds., *The Complete Greek Drama*. 2 vols. Random House, 1938.

SCIENCE

Cohen, M. R. and I. E. Drabkin, *A Source Book in Greek Science*. Harvard University Press, 1959.
Hippocrates. 4 vols. Transl. by W.H.S. Jones (Loeb Classical Library). Harvard University Press, 1957.
Taylor, Henry O., *Greek Biology and Medicine*. Cooper Square Publishers, 1963.

RELIGION AND MYTHOLOGY

*Hamilton, Edith, *Mythology*. Little, Brown, 1942.
Larousse Encyclopedia of Mythology. Putnam, 1959.
†Nilsson, Martin P., *Greek Folk Religion*. Harper & Row, 1961.

ATHLETICS AND FESTIVALS

Gardiner, E. N., *Athletics of the Ancient World*. Oxford University Press, 1930.
Gardiner, E. N., *Greek Athletic Sports and Festivals*. Macmillan, 1910.
Gardiner, E. N., *Olympia: its History and Remains*. Oxford University Press, 1925.

ALEXANDER AND THE HELLENISTIC WORLD

†Burn, A. R., *Alexander the Great and the Hellenistic Empire*. Collier, 1962.
Lamb, Harold, *Alexander of Macedon*. Doubleday, 1946.
The Cambridge Ancient History, Vol. VI, *Macedon 401-301 B.C.* Macmillan, 1927.
Robinson, C. A. Jr., *Alexander the Great*. E. P. Dutton, 1947.
†Tarn, W. W., *Alexander the Great*. Vols. I and II. Beacon Press, 1956.
Tarn, W. W., *The Greeks in Bactria and India*. Cambridge University Press, 1951.
*Tarn, W. W., and G. T. Griffith, *Hellenistic Civilization*. St. Martin's Press, 1952.

ACKNOWLEDGMENT OF QUOTATIONS

All quotations from Herodotus' *The Persian Wars* are from *The Greek Historians* Vol. I, Random House, 1942. Translation by George Rawlinson. All quotations from Thucydides' *The Peloponnesian War* are from the translation by Rex Warner, Penguin Books, 1961. *Other quotations:*
p. 33: Hesiod: from *The Oxford Book of Greek Verse in Translation*, Oxford University Press, 1944. Translation by Jack Lindsay. p. 39: Homer, *The Iliad*: translation by W.H.D. Rouse, Mentor Books, 1962, by arrangement with Thomas Nelson and Sons, Ltd., 1938. p. 43: *Ibid.* p. 55: Archilochus: first quotation from *The Cambridge Ancient History*, Vol. IV, *The Persian Empire and the West*, Macmillan, 1926. Second quotation from *Greek Civilization: From the Iliad to the Parthenon*, by André Bonnard, Macmillan, 1957.

p. 57: Alcman: from *The Oxford Book of Greek Verse in Translation*. Translation by Gilbert Highet. p. 78: Aeschylus, *The Persians*: from *The Complete Greek Drama*, Vol. I, Random House, 1938. Translation by Robert Potter. p. 95: Euripides: from *The Greek Way*, by Edith Hamilton, Mentor Books, 1963, by arrangement with W. W. Norton & Co., 1942. p. 101: Euripides, *The Trojan Women*: from *The Complete Greek Drama*, Vol. I. Translation by Gilbert Murray. p. 123: Sophocles, *Oedipus at Colonus*: from *The Complete Greek Tragedies*, Vol. III (Sophocles I), Modern Library. Translation by Robert Fitzgerald, copyrighted 1941 by Harcourt, Brace & World. p. 144: Demosthenes, "First Philippic": from *Demosthenes I*, The Loeb Classical Library, Harvard University Press, 1954. Translation by J. H. Vince.

ACKNOWLEDGMENTS

The editors of this book are particularly indebted to Cornelius Vermeule, Curator, Department of Classical Art, Museum of Fine Arts, Boston; Daniel E. Gershenson, Assistant Professor, Department of Classics, Columbia University; Brian F. Cook, Assistant Curator, Department of Greek and Roman Art, Metropolitan Museum of Art, New York; Gjon Mili; John Kondis, General Director of Archaeology, Athens; Henry S. Robinson, Director, and Eugene Vanderpool, American School of

Classical Studies at Athens; Homer A. Thompson, Field Director, John Travlos, Dorothy Burr Thompson, Poly Demoulini and Lucy Talcott, Agora Excavations, Athens; Christos Karouzos, General Ephor of Antiquities, Athens; Semni Karouzou, General Ephor of Antiquities, Athens; Nikolaos Platon, Director, Acropolis Museum, Athens; Vasileios Callipolitis, Director, Barbara Philippaki and Maria Petropoulakou, National Archaeological Museum, Athens; Emil Kunze, Director, and Gerhard Neumann, German Archaeological Institute, Athens; Mario Moretti, Superintendent, and Giovanni Scichilone, Museo Nazionale di Villa Giulia, Rome; Alfonso de Franciscis and Giuseppe Maggi, Museo Nazionale, Naples; Erminia Speyer, Vatican Galleries and Museums; Nina Longobardi and Ernest Nash, American Academy, Rome; Theodor Kraus, Istituto Archaeologico Germanico, Rome; Denys Haynes, Keeper of Greek and Roman Antiquities, British Museum, London; Gerhard R. Meyer, Director, and Elisabeth Rhode, Antikenabteilung, Staatliche Museen, East Berlin; Norbert Kunisch, Antikenabteilung, Staatliche Museen, West Berlin; Erwin M. Auer, Kunsthistorisches Museum, Vienna; Antikensammlungen, Prinz Carl Palais, Munich; The Rev. Raymond V. Schoder, S.J., Loyola University, Chicago; Phillip Bacon, Professor of Geography, Teachers College, Columbia University; Paul P. Vouras, Associate Professor of Geography, and Livio C. Stecchini, Assistant Professor of History, Paterson State College; Colonel John R. Elting, Acting Deputy Head, Department of Military Art and Engineering, and Frederick P. Todd, Director of the Museum, United States Military Academy, West Point; and Judy Higgins.

PICTURE CREDITS

The sources for the illustrations in this book are set forth below. Descriptive notes on the works of art are included. Credits for pictures positioned from left to right are separated by semicolons, from top to bottom by dashes. Photographers' names which follow a descriptive note appear in parentheses. Abbreviations include c. for century and ca. for circa.

Cover—Poseidon, bronze, ca. 460 B.C. (sometimes identified as Zeus), National Archaeological Museum, Athens (Gjon Mili).

CHAPTER 1: 10—Athena, bronze, ca. 350 B.C., Piraeus Museum (Roloff Beny). 12—Attic Geometric vase, detail, 8th c. B.C., The Metropolitan Museum of Art, Rogers Fund, 1914. 13—*Kouros* (youth), marble, 7th c. B.C., The Metropolitan Museum of Art, Fletcher Fund, 1932; Hermes by Praxiteles, marble, ca. 325 B.C., Olympia Museum (Nic Stournaras). 14, 15—Gems, impressions, 5th c. B.C., Museum of Fine Arts, Boston (John McQuade). 16, 17—Olympian Gods, marble, possibly 1st c. B.C., South Italy, Walters Art Gallery, Baltimore. 19—Apollo, bronze, ca. 530 B.C., National Archaeological Museum, Athens (Carlo Bavagnoli), 20—Amphora, clay, 5th c., B.C., Agora Museum in the Stoa of Attalos, Athens (Gjon Mili). 21—Temple of Athena, Lindos, Rhodes, 4th c. B.C., portico, ca. 200 B.C. (Sante Forlano). 22, 23—Siphnian Treasury, Delphi, marble frieze, ca. 525 B.C., Delphi Museum (Gjon Mili). 24—Nike of Samothrace (Winged Victory), marble, ca. 200 B.C., Louvre Museum, Paris (Gjon Mili). 25—Stele, Law against Tyranny, 336 B.C., marble, Agora Museum, Athens (Gjon Mili). 26, 27—Aristotle, Roman copy of 4th c. B.C. original, Museo Nazionale delle Terme, Rome (Gjon Mili)—Parthenon frieze, marble, completed 432 B.C., British Museum, London (Gjon Mili). 28—Jockey, bronze, ca. 150 B.C., National Archaeological Museum, Athens (Stephanos Papadopoulos). 29—Charioteer, bronze, ca. 470 B.C., Delphi Museum (George Hoyningen-Huene from Rapho-Guillumette; flexichrome by Peter Bitlisian).

CHAPTER 2: 30—Wall painting, Tiryns, 13th c. B.C., National Archaeological Museum, Athens (Stephanos Papadopoulos). 33—Temple of Ramses III, 12th c. B.C., Medinet Habu, Egypt (Eliot Elisofon). 36—Etruscan Bucchero vase, 7th c. B.C., The Metropolitan Museum of Art, Fletcher Fund, 1924 (Eric Schaal). 39 through 47 (except 41 and 44 below)—Sandstone frieze from Gjölbaschi, ca. 400 B.C., Kunsthistorisches Museum, Vienna (Erich Lessing from Magnum). 41—Walls of Troy (Ara Güler). 44—Samothrace (Roloff Beny).

CHAPTER 3: 48—Tholos, Delphi, ca. 400 B.C. (Gjon Mili). 54, 55—Silver stater from Phaselis, ca. 360 B.C.—silver octodrachma, Abdera, ca. 520-492 B.C.—silver tetradrachma, Syracuse, ca. 413 B.C.—silver stater, Abydos, ca. 390 B.C.—silver tetradrachma, Cyrene, ca. 435-375 B.C.; Athenian coins, silver, ca. 490-450 B.C., Museum of Fine Arts, Boston (John McQuade). 56, 58—Drawings by Victor and Maria Lazzaro. 61—Richard Meek. 62, 63—Richard Meek except left; Attic black-figured cup by Tleson, son of Nearchos, ca. 550 B.C., Trustees of the British Museum, London. 64, 65—Gjon Mili; calf-bearer, marble, ca. 560 B.C., Acropolis Museum, Athens (Gjon Mili)—Roloff Beny, Richard Meek. 66, 67—Gjon Mili, Poseidon, bronze, ca. 460 B.C., National Archaeological Museum, Athens (Gjon Mili).

CHAPTER 4: 68—Apulian red-figured krater by the Darius Painter, 4th c. B.C., Museo Nazionale, Naples (Emmett Bright). 70, 71—Corinthian helmet, bronze, 6th c. B.C.; lance, bronze, 5th c. B.C.—battering ram, bronze, 5th c. B.C., Olympia Museum (Deutsches Archäologisches Institut, Athens). 74, 75—Drawing by Victor and Maria Lazzaro. 77—Confucius from a Manchu stele (Brown Brothers). 79—Stele, 5th c. B.C., Kerameikos Museum, Athens (David Lees). 80—Attic white-ground jug, ca. 440 B.C., The Metropolitan Museum of Art, Fletcher Fund, 1937 (Eric Schaal); terra cotta from Tanagra, 5th c. B.C., British Museum, London (Raymond V. Schoder, S.J.)—terra cotta from Athens, 5th c. B.C., British Museum, London (Derek Bayes). 81—Stele of Panaitios, 4th c. B.C., National Archaeological Museum, Athens (Emile). 82, 83—Attic red-figured cup by Douris, ca. 480 B.C., Staatliche Museen, Berlin, Antikenabteilung—Attic red-figured cup, ca. 480 B.C., Museum of Fine Arts, Boston (Raymond V. Schoder, S.J.). 84—David Lees; pottery, 5th c. B.C., courtesy Agora Museum, Athens. 85—Terra cotta from Tanagra, 3rd c. B.C., Archaeological Museum, Leiden (Raymond V. Schoder, S.J.). 86—Attic black-figured jug, ca. 550 B.C., attributed to the Amasis Painter, The Metropolitan Museum of Art, Fletcher Fund, 1931 (Eric Schaal)—Attic black-figured vase by the Eucharides Painter, 5th c. B.C., Ashmolean Museum, Oxford; Apulian krater by the Statue Painter, 4th c. B.C., The Metropolitan Museum of Art, Rogers Fund, 1950 (Eric Schaal). 87—Attic black-figured jug, ca. 540 B.C., Museum of Fine Arts, Boston (Edward J. Moore). 88, 89—Attic black-figured cup, ca. 530 B.C., Louvre Museum, Paris (Chuzeville from Rapho-Guillumette); Attic black-figured amphora attributed to the Taleides Painter, ca. 550 B.C., The Metropolitan Museum of Art, purchase 1947, Joseph Pulitzer Bequest (Eric Schaal)—Attic black-figured cup by Nikosthenes as Potter, ca. 520 B.C., Louvre Museum, Paris (Heinz Zinram). 90, 91—Attic red-figured cup, ca. 460 B.C., Museo di Villa Giulia, Rome (Emmett Bright)—Attic red-figured jug, ca. 430 B.C., The Metropolitan Museum of Art, Fletcher Fund, 1937 (Eric Schaal); terra cotta relief from Melos, 5th c. B.C., Louvre Museum, Paris (Raymond V. Schoder, S.J.).

CHAPTER 5: 92—Detail of Parthenon, built 447-432 B.C. (Roloff Beny). 94—Drawings by Victor and Maria Lazzarro, Adapted from *Furniture of Ancient Greece* by T. H. Robsjohn-Gibbings and Carlton W. Pullin, by permission of Alfred A. Knopf, Inc. and from drawings copyrighted by C. P. Putnam's Sons in *Everyday Things in Ancient Greece* by Marjorie and C.H.B. Quennell. 96—Attic cup, 5th c. B.C., Vatican Museum (Emmett Bright). 98, 99—Juror's ballots, 4th c. B.C.—sale record, 414-413 B.C.—Ostrakon, 5th c. B.C.; allotment tokens, ca. 450-430 B.C., Agora Museum, Athens (Agora Excavations, American School of Classical Studies, Athens). 103—Attic votive relief, marble, 4th c. B.C., National Archaeological Museum, Athens (Bettmann Archive). 105—Pericles, Roman copy of 5th c. B.C. original, British Museum, London (Heinz Zinram). 106, 107—Drawing by Victor and Maria Lazzaro. 108—Speaker's platform, Pnyx, 4th c. B.C. (Constantin Manos from Magnum)—*Kleroterion*, marble, 3rd c. B.C., Agora Museum, Athens (Agora Excavations, American School of Classical Studies, Athens). 109—Parthenon frieze, marble (Alison Frantz). 110—Erechtheum, built 421-406 B.C. (Roloff Beny). 111—Parthenon frieze, marble, Acropolis Museum, Athens (Gjon Mili). 112, 113—Parthenon frieze, marble, British Museum, London (Gjon Mili); Parthenon (Carone from Paris-Match). 114—Detail from Parthenon (Gjon Mili). 115—Parthenon interior reconstruction by Leo Kerz; sculpture by Louis di Valentin (Norman Snyder).

CHAPTER 6: 116—Krater from Vix, ca. 500 B.C., bronze, Musée Archéologique, Châtillon-sur-Seine, France (Raymond V. Schoder, S.J.). 122, 123—Drawings by Victor and Maria Lazzaro. 125—Panathenaic amphora by the Berlin Painter, 5th c. B.C., Museo Nazionale, Naples (Emmett Bright). 126, 127—Attic red-figured cup, ca. 510 B.C., Louvre Museum, Paris (Heinz Zinram); ruins of the Palaestra, 3rd c. B.C., Olympia (Gjon Mili). 128, 129—Richard Meek, Panathenaic amphora, 5th c. B.C., Trustees of the British Museum, London—Panathenaic amphora attributed to the Euphiletos Painter, ca. 530 B.C., The Metropolitan Museum of Art, Rogers Fund, 1914 (Eric Schaal). 130, 131—Attic red-figured cup, ca. 480 B.C., Staatliche Museen zu Berlin, Antikenabteilung; Attic red-figured cup by the Epiktetos Painter, ca. 510 B.C., Agora Museum, Athens (Stephanos Papadopoulos)—Attic black-figured hydria, 6th c. B.C., Trustees of the British Museum, London. 132, 133—Marble reliefs from statue base, ca. 500 B.C., National Archaeological Museum, Athens (David Lees). 134—David Lees, Panathenaic amphora attributed to Euphiletos Painter, ca. 530 B.C., The Metropolitan Museum of Art, Rogers Fund, 1914 (Eric Schaal). 135—Boy victor, bronze, 5th c. B.C., Glyptothek, Munich (C. H. Krüger-Moessner).

CHAPTER 7: 136—Venus de Milo, marble, early 1st c. B.C., Louvre Museum, Paris (Gjon Mili). 138—Warrior, bronze, 6th c. B.C., Wadsworth Atheneum, Hartford, J. P. Morgan Collection (Lee Boltin). 140-141—Bas relief, 2nd c. B.C., plaster copy, Capitoline Museum, Rome (Alinari). 143—Drawing by Victor and Maria Lazzaro. 145—Theater of Dionysus, Athens, 4th c. B.C. to 2nd c. A.D. (Gjon Mili). 146—Attic red-figured pointed amphora by the Kleophrades Painter, ca. 500 B.C., Glyptothek, Munich (C. H. Krüger-Moessner). 147—White-ground cup by the Brygos Painter, ca. 490 B.C., Museum Antiker Kleinkunst, Munich (Friedrich Rauch)—Attic black-figured amphora, 6th c. B.C., courtesy Musées Royaux d'Art et d'Histoire, Brussels (Raymond V. Schoder, S.J.). 148, 149—Theater at Epidaurus, 4th c. B.C. (Raymond V. Schoder, S.J.); Theater of Dionysus (Gjon Mili). 150, 151—Relief, marble, Roman copy of 3rd c. B.C. original, The Art Museum, Princeton University (Raymond V. Schoder, S.J.); tragic mask, terra cotta, ca. 400 B.C., Staatliche Museen zu Berlin, Antikensammlung (Gjon Mili); tragic mask, terra cotta, ca. 300 B.C., National Archaeological Museum, Athens (Stephanos Papadopoulos)—comic mask, terra cotta, 3rd c. B.C., National Archaeological Museum, Athens (Emile); comic mask, terra cotta, ca. 200 B.C., Museum of Fine Arts, Boston (Edward J. Moore). 152—Hellenistic statuettes from Tanagra, terra cotta, Staatliche Museen zu Berlin, Antikensammlung (Gjon Mili). 153—Statuette from Tanagra, terra cotta, ca. 300 B.C., Staatliche Museen zu Berlin, Antikensammlung (Gjon Mili). 154, 155—George Hoyningen-Huene from Rapho-Guillumette; Norman Snyder, courtesy Circle in the Square, New York.

CHAPTER 8: 156—Mosaic, Roman copy of Hellenistic painting of 4th c. B.C., Museo Nazionale, Naples (David Lees). 159—Palace at Persepolis, relief, 6th-5th c. B.C. (Dmitri Kessel). 165—Silver coin from Paeonia, ca. 340-286 B.C., British Museum, London (Heinz Zinram). 166—Laocoön, marble, 1st c. B.C., Vatican Collections, Belvedere, Rome (David Lees). 167—Statue, marble, Roman copy of 2nd c. B.C. original, Glyptothek, Munich. 168—Detail, Temple of Apollo, Didyma, 4th c. B.C. to 2nd c. A.D. (Roloff Beny)—Sarcophagus from Iasus, 2nd c. A.D., National Museum, Istanbul (Roloff Beny). 169—Palmyra (Roloff Beny). 170—Buddha, Gandhara School, stucco, 2nd to 6th c. A.D., Kabul Museum, Afghanistan (Frances Mortimer from Rapho-Guillumette). 171—James Burke—relief, grey schist, Gandhara School, 2nd c. A.D., National Museum of Pakistan, Karachi (Frances Mortimer from Rapho-Guillumette). 172—Theater at Side, 2nd c. A.D. (Roloff Beny). 173—Temple of Olympian Zeus, 174 B.C.-131 A.D. (Roloff Beny). 174, 175—Temple of Poseidon, Cape Sunium, ca. 440 B.C. (Roloff Beny).

Illustrations on pages 180 through 183 by Leo and Diane Dillon.

INDEX

This symbol in front of a page number indicates a photograph or painting of the subject mentioned.

āle, chảotic, câre, ădd, ảccount, ärm, ásk, sofả; ēve, êvent, ĕnd, silĕnt, makēr; īce,

āle, châotic, câre, ădd, ăccount, ärm, ȧsk, sofȧ; ēve, êvent, ēnd, silĕnt, makēr; ice,

PRODUCTION STAFF FOR TIME INCORPORATED

John L. Hallenbeck (Vice President and Director of Production), Robert E. Foy,
James P. Menton, Caroline Ferri and Robert E. Fraser
Text photocomposed under the direction of Albert J. Dunn and Arthur J. Dunn

xx

Printed by Fawcett • Haynes Printing Corporation, Rockville, Maryland
Bound by R. R. Donnelley & Sons Company, Crawfordsville, Indiana
Paper by The Mead Corporation, Dayton, Ohio
Cover materials by The Plastic Coating Corporation, Holyoke, Massachusetts,
and The Holliston Mills Inc., Norwood, Massachusetts